Management Accounting in Enterprise Resource Planning Systems

Management Accounting in Enterprise Resource Planning Systems

Severin Grabski
Michigan State University, USA

Stewart Leech
The University of Melbourne, Australia

Alan Sangster
Middlesex University, UK

AMSTERDAM • BOSTON • HEIDELBERG • LONDON • NEW YORK • OXFORD
PARIS • SAN DIEGO • SAN FRANCISCO • SINGAPORE • SYDNEY • TOKYO
CIMA Publishing is an imprint of Elsevier

CIMA Publishing is an imprint of Elsevier
Linacre House, Jordan Hill, Oxford OX2 8DP, UK
30 Corporate Drive, Suite 400, Burlington, MA 01803, USA

Copyright © 2009. Severin Grabski, Stewart Leech and Alan Sangster. All rights reserved.

The right of Severin Grabski, Stewart Leech and Alan Sangster to be identified
as the authors of this work has been asserted in accordance with the Copyright,
Designs and Patents Act 1988

No part of this publication may be reproduced, stored in a retrieval system or transmitted
in any form or by any means electronic, mechanical, photocopying, recording or otherwise
without the prior written permission of the publisher

Permissions may be sought directly from Elsevier's Science & Technology Rights
Department in Oxford, UK: phone (+44) (0) 1865 843830; fax (+44) (0) 1865 853333;
e-mail: permissions@elsevier.com. Alternatively you can visit the Science and Technology
Books website at www.elsevierdirect.com/rights for further information

Notice
No responsibility is assumed by the publisher for any injury and/or damage to persons or
property as a matter of products liability, negligence or otherwise, or from any use or
operation of any methods, products, instructions or ideas contained in the material herein.

British Library Cataloguing in Publication Data
A catalogue record for this book is available from the British Library

ISBN: 978-1-85617-679-8

For information on all CIMA publications
visit our website at www.elsevierdirect.com

Typeset by Macmillan Publishing Solutions
(www.macmillansolutions.com)

Transferred to Digital Printing in 2009

Working together to grow
libraries in developing countries

www.elsevier.com | www.bookaid.org | www.sabre.org

ELSEVIER   BOOK AID
            International   Sabre Foundation

Contents

Executive Summary vii
Acknowledgments ix

1. **Introduction** 1
2. **Background to the Study and Review of Prior Research** 5
   2.1   ERP success factors 6
   2.2   ERP failure factors 7
   2.3   Impacts of ERP implementations upon management accounting and upon management accountants 8
   2.4   Implementation success 11
3. **Research Methodology** 13
4. **Case Studies** 15
   Case A 17
   Case B 24
   Case C 35
   Case D 45
   Case E 53
   Case F 66
   Case G 77
   Lessons learnt 85
5. **The Motivations for ERP Deployment** 89
6. **The Role of Management Accountants in the ERP System Implementation Process** 93
7. **Advice for Management Accountants in ERP Systems: Implementation, Use and Post-implementation Issues** 95
   7.1   Guidance for management accountants 95
       7.1.1   ERP implementation guidance 97
       7.1.2   Monitoring and post-implementation issues 98
8. **The Impact of ERP Systems on Management Accountants and Their Work** 103
   8.1   The changing role of the management accountants 104
   8.2   Skills needed by management accountants in ERP environments 110

	8.3	General impact of ERP systems on the work of management accountants	113
9.	**Summary and Conclusions**		**117**

References   121

Appendices   125

Index   147

Executive Summary

This report provides insights into the changes resulting from the implementation of ERP systems on the work and behaviour of management accountants. Management accountants have typically been tasked to accumulate and track costs, to prepare budgets and prepare performance reports. Current evidence points to management accountants using traditional software (such as spreadsheets) for budgeting, ABC, balanced scorecards and other performance management techniques independent of, rather than integrated with ERP systems. We describe the ERP implementation at seven different organisations and the resultant impact on its management accountants. The organisations all had different levels of success in the implementation of their ERP systems, and they are from a wide variety of business sectors. We believe that most organisations and most management accountants will be able to read through the cases and pick out where their own organisation stands, and what it should do based upon the lessons we report.

How have management accountants adapted to the changes resulting from the implementation of ERP systems? Do the tasks performed by management accountants change based upon the relative success of the ERP implementation? Has ERP software replaced traditional software in an ERP environment or are management accountants still using spreadsheets and other traditional software?

This report focuses on the differential impacts of successful as compared to less-than-successful ERP system implementations on the role of management accountants. It identifies what changes should occur in the practice of management accounting as a result of the implementation of ERP packages and provides advice to management accountants whose organisations are undergoing an ERP implementation or re-implementation project.

The results of this study are important to management accountants as they examine where their organisation stands relative to others and relative to the improvements that could be attained with the implementation of an ERP system.

Highlights from the extensive findings include:

- When management accountants are involved in an ERP system implementation, there is an increased likelihood of the implementation being a success.
- The impact of the ERP system on the role of the management accountant is related to the perceived success of the system implementation, with more successful implementations exhibiting the more dramatic changes to the role.

- While all ERP implementations results in changes in the tasks performed by management accountants, a successful ERP implementation results in a significant change in the management accountant's tasks, they become business partners not just data providers.
- A successful ERP implementation results in both increases in data quality and quality of decision-making, and in additional time for management accountants to become involved in value-adding tasks rather than mundane data recording and information reporting tasks.
- Management accountants in an ERP environment needs a strong understanding of the business and the business processes, significant interpersonal skills, leadership skills, decision-making skills, analytical skills, planning skills and technical skills.
- The role of management accountants in an ERP environment is more that of a business advisor to top management than that of a traditional management accountant.

Acknowledgments

The research team would like to acknowledge the support of the Chartered Institute of Management Accountants (CIMA), who have provided the funding for this project.

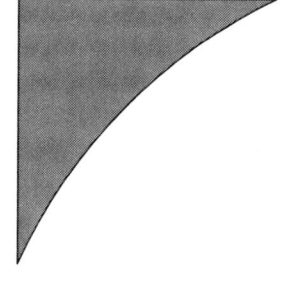

Chapter 1

Introduction

Enterprise resource planning (ERP) systems are becoming commonplace. Many studies report that about 90% of large business organisations have implemented an ERP system (Olhager and Selldin, 2003; Manufacturing Business Technology, 2008). In addition to their implementation in large enterprises, they are now implemented in many mid-sized organisations. At this time, the significant benefits that accrue to businesses that have successfully implemented ERP systems have been well documented. Yusuf et al. (2004) suggest that ERP systems offer three major benefits: (1) business process automation; (2) timely access to management information and (3) Improvement in the supply chain via the use of E-communication and E-commerce. Other benefits include information visibility, decreased costs, faster period-end closes, greater market responsiveness, better control over reverse logistics and others (e.g. Latamore, 1999; Davenport, 2000; Wallace and Kremzar, 2001; Cullen et al., 2007).

Some research is now beginning to appear that examines the effect of ERP systems on the people who use them (e.g. Granlund and Malmi, 2002; Lodh and Gaffikin, 2003; Scapens and Jazayeri, 2003). In particular, one group that is severely affected by the ERP systems is the management accountants.

Management accountants have typically been tasked to accumulate and track costs, to prepare budgets and performance reports. Current evidence points to management accountants using traditional software (such as spreadsheets) for budgeting, activity-based costing (ABC), balanced scorecards and other performance management techniques independent of, rather than integrated with ERP systems, despite many of these tasks having already been included in current ERP systems.

How have management accountants adapted to the changes resulting from the implementation of ERP systems? Do the tasks performed by management accountants change based upon the relative success of the ERP implementation? Has ERP software replaced traditional software in an ERP environment or are management accountants still using spreadsheets, etc.? There has been some research undertaken on the effects of ERP systems on management accountants and management control systems (see Fahy, 2000; Granlund and Malmi, 2002; Caglio, 2003; Gould, 2003; Hyvonen, 2003; Lodh and Gaffikin, 2003; Quattrone and Hopper, 2003; Scapens and Jazayeri, 2003). The early reports (e.g. Granlund and Malmi, 2002) are that there seems to be a decrease in the multiple data entries required compared with non-integrated accounting systems; however, the goal of having the management accountant becomes more of a business analyst has not occurred in the majority of cases.

The objective of this research project is to provide further insight into the changes resulting from the implementation of ERP systems on the work and behaviour of management accountants. This report presents our findings, focusing on the differential effects of successful as compared to less-than-successful ERP system implementations on the role of management accountants. Further, we seek to provide insight and advice to management accountants whose organisations are undergoing an ERP (re-) implementation project.

Some researchers (e.g. Caglio, 2003; Lodh and Gaffikin, 2003; Scapens and Jazayeri, 2003) argue that surveys that seek to identify the impact of ERP systems on the outcomes of the implementation process will not be able to address the complexities of the change process, and that longitudinal studies are required for that purpose. In this research we did not perform a longitudinal study, but addressed the time span issue through the design of the study.

Following three pilot case studies and responses to a postal questionnaire, an interview instrument was developed and used to conduct in-depth interviews at seven large organisations in the UK that had implemented ERP systems. In each organisation, we interviewed at least one member of the ERP implementation project team.

Although we cannot examine all of the nuances of the changes identified by the interviewees as having resulted from the ERP implementations, the interviews allow us to obtain a very good perspective of the changes that occur from implementations of this type and of how they impact both managerial accounting and the management accountant.

We agree with Scapens and Jazayeri (2003) that research should identify the opportunities created by the implementation of ERP systems for management accounting and the management accountant. We demonstrate from our findings that these opportunities are dependent upon the relative success of the ERP implementation.

Chapter 2

Background to the Study and Review of Prior Research

Many organisations have implemented ERP systems; however, the level of success associated with these systems has varied widely. In the late 1990s, many of these systems were implemented to eliminate the 'Y2K' crises. Unfortunately, some of these implementations only focused on replacing the financial reporting systems and ignored the benefits that could have been obtained through the design and implementation of a system that integrated the operations of the entire organisation (i.e. including accounting, manufacturing, supply chain management, etc.). The lack of integration and subsequent required upgrades (to ensure that the software will continue to be supported by the vendor), along with business combinations has resulted in most of the early ERP adopting firms re-implementing their ERP environments. Some were simply upgrades, whereas others were essentially a complete, new ERP implementation project.

It is commonly accepted by the business world that information technology should be viewed as more than just an automation of business processes; information technology can fundamentally change the way business is done. Many organisations, therefore, seek to improve their competitiveness by utilising advanced information technology, such as ERP systems. However, consistent with the argument made by Carr (2003), research indicates that organisations generally do not obtain any long-lived competitive advantage through an ERP system implementation, any benefit obtained is quickly competed away. However, this is not to say that organisations should not implement ERP systems – those that do not soon find themselves loosing ground to organisations that have successfully implemented these systems (Poston and Grabski, 2001; Hunton et al., 2003).

The implementation and subsequent operation of an ERP system is not an easy task. Without sound management of the implementation process, and without the identification of the changes an enterprise must undergo during operation, ERP systems can result in many difficulties for organisations (see Cameron and Meyer, 1998; Davenport, 1998; Deutsch, 1998). As argued in Grabski et al. (2001), ERP systems are different from traditional systems in scale, complexity, organisational impact, cost and subsequent business impact. ERP systems typically impact the entire organisation and are almost always associated with the business process re-engineering (Davenport, 2000).

Traditional analysis and design projects had minimal re-engineering and the software was written to match current processes, whereas ERP systems are implemented with minimal change to the software while significant re-engineering of business processes to match the ERP software occurs. Organisations that implement ERP must be ready to do so and many have run into difficulty because they were not organised in the correct fashion to benefit from the implementation (Yusuf et al., 2004). The costs associated with ERP systems are significantly higher than those of traditional systems and mistakes such as these can be extremely costly – for example, Dell Computers spent millions of dollars on an ERP system that had to be scrapped as it was too rigid for the expanding nature of the company (Turnick, 1999). In some cases, a failed implementation can destroy the organisation, as in the case of the FoxMeyer Drugs bankruptcy (Scott, 1999).

2.1 ERP success factors

Researchers have begun to identify the success factors associated with successful ERP system implementations. Early research into ERP implementation success factors (e.g. Holland and Light, 1999; Jarrar et al., 2000; Grabski et al., 2001; Somers and

Nelson, 2001; Akkermans and van Helden, 2002) generated lists of factors but did not provide any guidance as to whether all the factors were needed, or if all the factors needed to be used with the same level of effort. More recently, Aloini et al. (2007), emphasising the importance of organisations focusing on ways to make their ERP implementation successful, looked at different approaches taken in the literature and compared them from a risk management point of view to highlight the key risk of failure factors and their potential impact on ERP projects success.

Grabski and Leech (2007) extended the research on control theory (e.g. Ouchi, 1979; Eisenhardt, 1985, 1989; Kirsch, 1996, 1997; Kirsch et al., 2002) through the use of the economic theory of complementarities (see Milgrom and Roberts, 1990, 1994, 1995). The basic issue they explored was the limitation of a portfolio of controls that were hypothesised to be used in a singular fashion when complex projects demanded the use of multiple techniques simultaneously. They examined the risks and controls associated with ERP system implementations and developed critical success factors that when used together enhanced the outcomes. They found that all the factors were necessary, and that no one factor by itself was sufficient for a successful implementation.

Based upon a survey of organisations that implemented ERP systems, they were able to aggregate the specific individual factors identified in the prior research into five overarching factors:

1. project management,
2. change management,
3. alignment of the business with the information system,
4. oversight (internal audit) activities and
5. consultant and planning activities.

Numerous controls exist within each of the five overarching categories (and some controls applied across categories, consistent with the theory of complementarity). As a result, we now have a better understanding of the complexities associated with successful ERP implementations and why some organisations, while on the surface appear to be doing the prescribed steps, are missing out on important processes.

2.2 ERP failure factors

Concerning unsuccessful ERP implementations, Aloini et al. (2007) carried out a meta-analysis of published research since 1999 and concluded that there are four broad categories of ERP system failure:

1. **Process failure**, when the project is not completed within the time and budget.
2. **Expectation failure**, when the IT systems do not match user expectations.

3. **Interaction failure**, when users attitudes towards IT are negative.
4. **Correspondence failure**, when there is no match between IT systems and the planned objectives.

Within these categories, they identified 19 risk factors, which are consistent with those identified by Grabski and Leech (2007). These included, inadequate selection of the ERP project to adopt, low key user involvement, inadequate training and instruction, inadequate business process re-engineering and ineffective consulting services. ERP user groups, such as ERP-SELECT in 2004 (http://erp.ittoolbox.com/groups/vendor-selection/erp-select/eraselect-erp-for-university-587056)[1] have offered lists of the factors that may lead to failure of ERP implementations as follows:

- Education (not understanding what the new 'system' is designed to achieve).
- Lack of top management commitment (management being involved but not dedicated).
- Inadequate requirements definition (current processes are not adequately addressed).
- Poor ERP package selection (the package does not address the basic business functions of the client).
- Inadequate resources employed by the client.
- Internal resistance to changing the 'old' processes.
- A poor fit between the software and users procedures.
- Unrealistic expectations of the benefits and the return on investment (ROI).
- Inadequate training (users do not properly know how to use the new tool).
- Unrealistic time frame expectations.
- A bottom-up approach is employed (the process is not viewed as a top management priority).
- The client does not properly address and plan for the expenses involved.

2.3 Impacts of ERP implementations upon management accounting and upon management accountants

Research on the effects of ERP systems on management accounting (e.g. Booth et al., 2000; Granlund and Malmi, 2002; Caglio, 2003; Granlund and Mouritsen, 2003;

---

[1]Information correct as of 18 June 2008.

Hyvonen, 2003; Lodh and Gaffikin, 2003; Maccarone, 2000; Quattrone and Hopper 2003; Scapens and Jazayeri, 2003) suggests that ERP systems have little impact on management accounting, but that the management accountant is evolving into a business consultant (Caglio, 2003; Rom and Rohde, 2004).

Using a field study of 10 companies in Finland, Granlund and Malmi (2002) examined the effect of integrated enterprise–wide information systems on management accounting and management accountants' work. They concluded that '... *ERPS projects have led to relatively small changes in management accounting and control techniques*' (p. 299). Booth et al. (2000) also found similar results, as did Rom and Rohde (2004), who found that strategic enterprise management (SEM) systems had a positive impact on management accounting practices whereas ERP systems only had a positive impact on transactional management accounting (e.g. data collection).

Scapens and Jazayeri (2003) found that there was no fundamental change in the nature of management accounting information; however, there were changes in the role of management accountants. ERP systems reduced the routine work undertaken by accountants and led to the routinisation of accounting through evolutionary change. Management accountants and mangers found new ways of working with the ERP system, each performing different tasks than before, for example, operating managers can access the information themselves from the ERP system rather than waiting for the accounting report, and the management accountant performs more analysis of results than before.

Fahy (2000) also explored the implications of SEM software for management accounting and control activities. He concluded that '*SAP, Peoplesoft and ERP vendors appear to view SEM essentially as a technological issue rather than a management/decision support issue*'; and '*While SEM technologies will remain largely the domain of established enterprise systems vendors the successful implementation of SEM will require a much richer understanding of the nature of strategic management and an understanding of the decision support process.*'

Research into linking SEM, performance measurement and management (PMM) and organisational change programs (which could include ERP implementations) was examined by Brignall and Ballantine (2004). Although they agreed with Fahy that SEM implementations were generally treated as technology projects, successful adoption requires a broad perspective including the needs of the organisation. This is consistent with the requirement of a strategic perspective for the implementation of an ERP system, a necessary but not sufficient condition for a successful implementation (Grabski et al., 2001).

The use of ERP and 'Best of Breed' (BoB) systems in Finland was examined by Hyvonen (2003). Financial departments were more interested in the traditional BoB systems whereas other departments preferred the ERP solution. The preference for an ERP system also occurred when a strategic and technical solution was desired.

A partial explanation for the use of BoB in the financial area was offered – when managerial control–type solutions are introduced in the financial area, the concern is on how to best obtain the data and present the information to the relevant decision makers. This does not require an integrated system, and so facilitates a BoB-type choice. If a strategic, organisation-wide solution is desired, an ERP-type solution is chosen. Hyvonen found no differences (except for more budgeting problems for ERP adopters) between ERP and BoB systems with respect to data measurement, data collection and usability.

Both Fahy (2000) and Granlund and Malmi (2002) suggest that further research is required to provide a richer understanding of the use of ERP systems and related SEM technologies in management accounting, strategic management and decision support. Further evidence of the need for a comprehensive research study is provided by Fearon (2000) who concluded that '... *the majority of Canadian companies today continue to use the most cumbersome and uncollaborative tool for enterprise budgeting – the commercial spreadsheet.*' He urged the integration of the budgeting system with the integrated ERP system. Further, the ERP system is seen as the basis for a successful balanced scorecard approach (Edwards, 2001). The balanced scorecard, with data obtained from the ERP system provides management with visibility into the business units and the ability to monitor progress against the overall organisation plan.

Wallace and Kremzar (2001) suggest that the two critically important objectives for ERP system implementations are fact transfer and behaviour change. Examples given of fact transfer relevant to management accounting include, '*when the cost accounting manager learns about ERP's extremely high requirements for inventory record accuracy*' (p. 138). An example of behaviour change is '*when the manager leads the charge to eliminate the annual physical inventory, because he or she knows that inventory records sufficiently accurate for successful ERP are more than accurate for balance sheet valuation – and that physical inventory cost time and money but often degrade inventory accuracy*' (p. 138). These examples provide some insight into the impacts that ERP systems may have upon management accountants.

A model of the impact of ERP systems on management accounting and management accountants was developed by Granlund and Malmi (2002). They proposed that ERP systems have both a direct and indirect effect on management accountants and management accounting systems. Examples of direct effects are changes in report content, timing, scheduling, etc. that are caused by the ERP system. Indirect effects result from changed management practices, changes in business processes, etc. that are initiated by the ERP implementation. This model, informed by other researchers (Booth et al., 2000; Caglio, 2003; Granlund and Malmi, 2002; Granlund and Mouritsen, 2003; Hyvonen, 2003; Lodh and Gaffikin, 2003; Maccarone, 2000; Scapens and Jazayeri, 2003) forms the basis for our research and is presented in Figure 2.1.

Background to the Study and Review of Prior Research

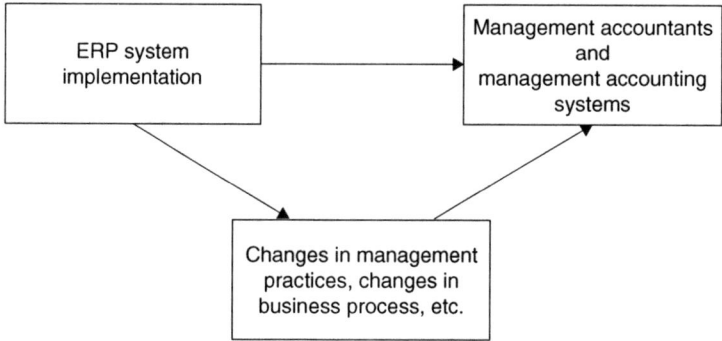

Figure 2.1 Impact of ERP systems on management accountants and management accounting. *Source*: Granlund and Malmi (2002).

2.4 Implementation success

One element perhaps surprisingly not identified in this model is the success of the ERP implementation. It would seem likely that any assessment of the success of any ERP project would be related to the changes resulting from the ERP project, and that the impact upon management accountants would be related to the success of the implementation. A successful implementation would be expected to free management accountants to do other things and to move them in the direction of becoming business consultants. A less successful ERP project might increase their activity on some of their existing tasks, absorbing any time saved through their being required to spend less time on other tasks, leaving no time for them to develop into business consultants.

It is possible that an ERP system could be implemented without any change actually occurring because it does nothing different – the management accountants still need to retrieve the data and prepare reports using some other (e.g. spreadsheet) software, which may either have been intended in the implementation or not. If it was the latter, this would give grounds for viewing the implementation as a failure – there has been no impact of the implementation upon the management accountants, yet there should have been one.

Alternatively, there could be no change because everything was already done by a system in place and all that has occurred is that, for example, different ERP software is now being used to perform the same processes as before and the switch of system was a success. In this case, very little change would be expected in the role of the management accountants. However, if the implementation failed, significant changes may be expected in the role of the management accountants.

From an economic perspective, a straight replacement of one ERP system with another does not seem as likely as the implementation of an ERP system that mimics a legacy system. An organisation will not spend millions and incur significant disruption if a system is already in place. However, the replacement of an ERP system due to removal of vendor support, or acquisition by an organisation that uses a different ERP solution and a mandated change to that solution are possible reasons for switching to different ERP software, both of which are economically defensible.

In this study, we adjusted Granlund and Malmi's model to include the success of the ERP implementation. As objective measures of ERP system success are generally not available, perceived success was used: business managers (including IT executives, management accountants, and auditors) generally are able to provide an indication of the system's relative success (i.e. if no one can obtain the needed information to run the business, they will know this and state that the ERP system is not successful; if they can obtain in-depth reports cutting across functional areas in a real-time basis, and have real-time information on inventory and production levels, they will state that the ERP system is successful; hard metrics are not required for this assessment).

If an ERP system implementation is successful, the focus of the organisation changes from a functional orientation to a process orientation (Davenport, 2000; Wallace and Kremzar, 2001). Doing so requires a change in the management and accounts reporting structure; a change in the generation of reports (since all data are now obtained from a centralised database); and a requirement for communication across functional areas. Since management accountants no longer need to generate the 'ordinary' reports, they can provide value for the organisation through the generation of forward-looking reports and improved analyses of business options. This is similar to what Caglio (2003) referred to as the 'hybridisation' of management accountants. Alternatively, if management accountants insist upon continuing to generate reports outside the ERP system similar to those produced automatically within the ERP system (and the ERP system would generate these reports in a more timely manner), the management accountants will not provide any additional value to that provided by the ERP system and their role will be threatened.

This project examined the changes resulting from the implementation of ERP packages on the practice of management accounting. It identified what other changes should occur in the practice of management accounting as a result of the implementation of ERP packages. The results of this study are important to management accountants, not only for these two elements but also when they examine where their organisation stands relative to others and relative to the improvements that could be attained from an effective ERP system.

Research Methodology

Chapter 3

A multistep research plan was utilised. The plan comprised of the following:

1. Preparation of an interview script that was informed by prior research (Grabski et al., 2001) to be used for preliminary interviews with management accountants, information system professionals and supervisory personnel.
2. These interviews informed the development of a questionnaire to be sent out to CIMA members.
3. Sending out the questionnaires and analysing the responses.

4. Creation of a structured interview script, based upon the responses obtained in the mail-out survey. This script was used in a series of in-depth interviews conducted across a variety of organisations that had experienced differing degrees of success in the implementation and use of ERP systems (described in Chapter 4 of this report).

The preliminary interviews were conducted with three different companies in 2003 and involved six individuals (four individuals from one company and one each from the other companies). All interviews were recorded with the interviewees' consent, and the interviewees were informed that they could end the interview at any time.

The postal questionnaire was then developed based upon prior research and the interviews. The questionnaire (Appendix 4) and associated information sheet (Appendix 3) were mailed out in early January 2004 to CIMA members along with a covering letter from CIMA informing the participants of the objective of the research and the importance of responding (Appendix 2). All respondents were provided with postage paid envelopes so that they could complete and submit their questionnaire independent of any other respondent.

By the end of February 2004, 16 replies to the first mailing had been received from 14 different companies. As per normal postal survey research practice, a second (and final) mailing of the questionnaires was sent on 3 March 2004. After the two mailings, 22 responses were received. These responses informed the development of the interview script used in the subsequent case studies.

The intensive case studies involved visiting seven organisations during a 2-week period in September 2004. Structured interviews (using an interview script developed following analysis of the responses to the postal questionnaire – see Appendix 6) were conducted and 12 individuals were interviewed. The organisations were all located in various cities across England. As in the preliminary interviews, these interviews were recorded with the consent of the interviewees and all participants were informed that they could end the interview at any time.

Chapter 4

Case Studies

This chapter starts by presenting seven case studies in which the impact of the implementation of an ERP system on the Management Accountant is examined. These case studies provide a robust setting. The companies are primarily large, publicly traded organisations from a wide variety of industries and are summarised in Table 4.1. Some have been very successful in their ERP implementation whereas others are still trying to find value in these systems.

Table 4.1 Company and industry

Company	Industry
AAA	Telecommunications
BBB	Heavy engineering and chemicals
CCC	Audio and telecommunications production and distribution
DDD	Food services and beverages
EEE	Food and consumer products
FFF	Automotive
GGG	Energy/aerospace

The names of all organisations and the parties involved in each case study have been changed so as to preserve anonymity.

Case A

This company (referred to as AAA) is a large organisation operating in the telecommunications industry and is part of a much larger multinational corporation in related industries. The Senior Manager involved in the ERP system implementation describes the case. All quoted comments are from this senior manager.

Background

AAA works with customers on relevant design, construction, operations and management of their telecommunications systems.

In 1999, the company implemented JD Edwards (JDE) ERP system. The full-time project team of 8 people included a Management (Project) Accountant (hereafter Management Accountant). The modules implemented included financials, distribution and supply chain. A motivation for the implementation of the ERP system was the Year 2000 problem.

The Managing Director (MD) sponsored and backed the ERP implementation and played a vital role in ensuring that the implementation ran smoothly. If a major problem occurred during the implementation with either people or process, the MD was called upon to find the solution. This ensured that the people and process changes were implemented smoothly and contributed to the success of the new system.

The ERP system is process-oriented and the company organisation varies between process-oriented and business function-oriented depending on the department. In answer to the question, '*To what extent does the ERP system and the organisation structure match?*', the response was '*You would put it midway at the moment.*' (Point 4 on a scale of 1–7, where 1 is no match and 7 is a perfect match.)

The main task of the Management (and other) Accountants with the ERP system implementation was the creation of the structure of the Chart of Accounts. They built a level of detail that resulted in a six-level structure in the Chart of Accounts. This allows the Management Accountants to drill down to the appropriate level to ascertain project costs. They were responsible for designing the Chart of Accounts around both the business reporting requirements, and reporting how well the organisation was doing financially. The developed Chart of Accounts provides the ability to assess the profit/loss in a project at a detailed level. (The example used was: '*What is the amount of money that we have spent on one contractor to do a certain job?*') 'So the [Management Accountants] have had to ... design a matrix of a combination of

18 Management Accounting in Enterprise Resource Planning Systems

the financial view and the business view to give us hopefully a Chart of Accounts which, at the level of detail they have gone to, will allow us to do that.'

In answer to the question *'What would the Management Accountants do differently/ the same knowing everything they know now after the ERP implementation?'*, the response was, *'They would certainly go about designing the structure of the Chart of Accounts the same way, but they would try and simplify the structure. There is duplication within the structure because of the way they did it by division, then by region and then by project. They would now start with the projects and built up into region and division. As it is, the project is almost a sub-set of everything else, rather than [the project] should be driving it. [This would] probably be much simpler.'*

The ERP system provides the numbers and the basic reports. For presentation purposes, the numbers are automatically downloaded into Excel spreadsheets (using macros) to provide the level of presentation required. This allows the use of the graphics and other presentation facilities within Excel. Excel is used now only as a presentation tool and not as a reporting tool. Prior to the ERP system, spreadsheets were used for reporting.

The implementation was assisted by a team of three full-time external consultants, who continued throughout and for 1-month's reporting after implementation.

The ERP implementation was seen as very successful for the following reasons:

(a) There is a reduction in inventory levels.
(b) The monthly accounts are now closing in 2 days (rather than 10 days prior to the ERP system).
(c) Financial accuracy and financial efficiency has significantly improved.
(d) Reports are being produced that the business understands and the business 'actually work to and it is only one number.'
(e) 'Procurement now use workflow to determine who has raised the requisition, when they raised it, what the value is, who has authorised it…'
(f) 'The stock control people now understand what we have in stock and they understand we have something like 4500 sites where we have equipment throughout the UK.' (There are about 250,000 items bar-coded.)

The role of the Management Accountants

As reported earlier, a Management Accountant was a full-time member of the project team, actively involved in the implementation of the ERP system. Currently, there are 13 Management Accountants in the company, which includes 4 assigned to regions and employed on projects and a central reporting team of 4 Management Accountants that undertake end-of-month reporting and reporting throughout the monthly periods.

Use of the system by the Management Accountants

It is estimated that about 90–95% of work performed by the Management Accountants relies on the new system.

The changing role of the Management Accountants

'Their role has changed almost 180 degrees because whereas before they were relied upon to be the calculating engine to provide the reports, now they are more interpreters and navigators.'

Other staff are now responsible for entering project data, the Project Manager is responsible for ensuring that the time sheets are completed and for time and costs allocated to a project. The Management Accountants on a project now examine the project timelines, the profitability of the project and *'…spending their time doing management appraisal of the projects rather than just generating the numbers.'* They are now monitoring the project as it proceeds and recommending appropriate action rather than gathering data and not knowing the outcome until after the project is finished.

With the implementation of the new system, Management Accountants are now assigned to regions rather than being located at Head Office. The number of Management Accountants has increased slightly due to this regionalisation.

With the new ERP system, the data is now collected from the source. The Management Accountants are now interpreting the data rather than having to be responsible to ensure that the data is collected. Prior to the ERP system implementation, they *'…spent most of their time running around trying to find out where the data was.'* The responsibility for data entry into the ERP system is now the responsibility of the Project Manager and/or Procurement. Management now relies on the Management Accountants to interpret the numbers and to *'tell them what is going on.'*

The extent to which the new system has had an impact on the role of Management Accountants on the following functions was described as follows:

The scores relate to the question: 'On a scale from 1 to 7 (1: very much reduced to 7: very much increased).'

(a) *Time spent on data collection* 'Very much gone down'	**Score = 2**
(b) *Time spent on data analysis* 'A lot more'	**Score = 6**
(c) *Involvement in business decision-making* 'Very much gone up'	**Score = 6**

(d) *Focus on internal reporting, for example performance measurement and control issues*   Score = 5

'Yes, they do a lot more...'

(e) *Focus on external environment (e.g. benchmarking)*   Score = N/A

'We don't really do that. Because of the industry we are in, we are telecommunications...so we don't really benchmark from that point of view.' (It should be noted that the company has a large market share.)

The following summarises the response to the questions listed below:

(a) *To what extent are traditional analysis performed that focus on past operating results compared to decision support type of analysis that have a forward-looking focus?*

The Management Accountants use historical data only to help forecast what is going to happen. They are more concerned with the future of a project to ensure that it is profitable.

Since they analyse and investigate historical data to determine future outcomes, it was estimated that about 50% of the time spent on backward-looking analysis and 50% is spent on forward-looking analysis. Prior to the implementation of the ERP system, most of the time was spent on historical/backward-looking data – '*probably 80–85% historical.*' It is a lot easier to undertake the forward-looking work with the new system.

(b) *Are the Management Accountants performing cross-functional analysis compared to domain specific analysis?*

Before the implementation of the new system, the data wasn't available to undertake cross-functional analysis. The Management Accountants are now involved in cross-functional analysis – there are third party contractors, procurement, maintenance, asset management and '*Commercial, who say how much it is going to cost and that is how much we are going to make on it. That is totally across the business.*'

It was noted that the Management Accountants are taking both a '*project view*' and '*business view.*'

(c) *Since less time is needed for data capture and less time is spent generating routine reports for managers, what are the Management Accountants doing with the extra time?*

The Management Accountants are spending a lot of time attending customer meetings and actually dealing with customers. They provide '*a reality check*' to the promises made by the Sales team. They provide the business unit heads with forecasts of activity in the next 3 months – forecasts are vital to the business when there are approximately 6000 projects. Before the implementation of the new system, it was very difficult to manage 6000 projects. The Management Accountants are now '... *on top of the projects.*'

They can forecast how many projects are going to close 3 months ahead. '*This is the kind of work that they do now and it is very much not an end-of-month exercise anymore. Whereas, before [the implementation of the new system], it was always getting everything together so that we can report it at the end of the month. Now on a daily basis, they are looking at what is happening in the business.*'

In summary, the Management Accountants are involved in discussion with the business management team as to the progress-to-date on projects – is it profitable; what parts of the project are profitable and are the projects on time?

'*It is a massive change for them and it has taken them away from the old fashioned financial everybody works hard at the month-end, and comes in on a Saturday and Sunday, and then rushing around to try and get ready for the next month-end. A different concept.*'

(d) *Has the formal or informal communication structure involving the Management Accountants changed as a result of the new system implementation?*

The communication has expanded because of the way Management Accountants are now involved in discussions with the business management team. '*Whether it is more formal or not is difficult to say, I think it is a company culture thing rather than a Management Accountant thing. We are in a fast moving industry, things change so rapidly a lot of what we do is informal.*'

(e) *How satisfied were the Management Accountants, both prior to and post the new system implementation?*

Before the implementation of the new system, there was turnover of about 1 every 6 months amongst the Management Accountants. Since the implementation, there has been no turnover in the past 3 years.

(f) *How have the Management Accountants contributed to the success of the new system?*

Although it was difficult to isolate the contribution alone of the Management Accountants, '*the more [they] understood, the more it was going to do for them, the more involved they became the more positive they became and... they were probably were one of the big change agents. They were very much part of "the business up to now has been doing this, now it is going to do that" – they were really in the forefront of change.*'

If the Management Accountants had resisted the changes, the new system would still have been successful but to a lesser degree. The company would still be better at procurement and managing the maintenance of the sites, '*but not as good at working out whether or not we are going to make any money.*'

The changing role of the Management Accountant in successful/unsuccessful implementations

The role of the Management Accountant is very different in successful implementations as compared to unsuccessful implementations.

'...*if you are successful and you build the foundation on which the Management Accountant can build, then that is very vital. I think the Management Accountant now, given a successful ERP system behind him, can get into the business and actually do the job. If he has to remain inside Finance, picking the bones out of an unsuccessful ERP system and putting that together, then he is struggling.*'

Recommendations for Management Accountants

The following summarises the responses to the questions (listed below) about recommendations for Management Accountants involved in the implementation and use of ERP systems.

(a) *What skills would you recommend for Management Accountants that have recently implemented ERP systems?*
- Analytical skills
- Communication skills
- Understanding the business
  - 'Where is the money going to?'
  - 'Where would I spend it?'
  - 'Where the business is going?'
  - 'Where the business makes money?'
  - 'Where [does the business] get the biggest benefit?'
- Presentation skills
- Entrepreneurial salesman skills

The Management Accountants must be able to communicate with the Management team and explain the financial data, and the impact and consequences of the financial data. '*So the skills are very much communication and very much business sense and understanding.*'

(b) *What is the best practice for a Management Accountant working with this type of system?*

Attend customer and/or business meetings and demonstrate what a Management Accountant does and how he performs. The Management Accountant in an ERP environment needs to inform customer and business meetings. '*People in a business will treat the financial department the way that the financial department presents itself. If the financial department sits in the corner and throws bits of paper out with numbers on, then the business will treat them like that. If the financial department goes out into the business and sells itself and says, "Look what I can do for you", then the business will respond to it.'*

For a new Management Accountant, an efficient induction to the way the job is done is vital.

Summary

In this company the implementation was very successful. A Management Accountant was part of the project team of eight people. Since the implementation, the turnover of Management Accountants has ceased, indicating an increase in job satisfaction. The role of the Management Accountants has changed substantially. They are now responsible for monitoring and managing projects and forecasting results. They are heavily involved with both customers and management. Their role has changed from one of data collection and month-end reporting to being heavily involved in business decision-making.

The recommended skills set for Management Accountants in this ERP environment include good communication skills, being entrepreneurial in selling their message to customers and management, and being able to advise on projects and business decisions. Software skills were not seen as any more important than in a non-ERP environment.

Case B

The interviewee was a Senior Executive of a firm of Management Consultants that works with organisations that are going through large technology-driven change programmes. The Management Consultant described the experiences of one large listed company (referred to as BBB). All comments concerning post-implementation relate to one specific business unit of BBB, and all quotes are from the Management Consultant.

Background

THE MANAGEMENT CONSULTANTS

The companies with which the Management Consultants work are often undertaking significant ERP implementations, where the scope of organisational and process change required to deliver tangible benefit is significant. In the majority of cases, the ERP software involved has been *SAP*, but the Management Consultants have also been involved with other ERP software implementations, such as *Oracle* and *Peoplesoft*.

The Management Consultants usually work with the business alongside a technical implementation partner to ensure that it is ready and able to adopt the new ways of working demanded by the new system. That is, the Management Consultants focus upon managing the organisational and process impacts of the implementation. As such, it is in an excellent position to assess the effect of ERP systems on the management accounting function within its client organisations.

The Company (BBB)

BBB is a heavy-engineering/chemicals company. It is a plc and is subdivided into a number of reporting units.

In the late 1990s, BBB plc decided that it wanted to sell-off one of its main reporting units, which at the time consisted of six individual business units. Although part of a single reporting unit, these six business units all operated slightly differently from each other and had different accounting systems and processes based on legacy systems. The legacy systems were considered seriously at risk because of the *millennium bug.* In addition to the obvious concern about the risk to ongoing operations that this posed, BBB was concerned that the outdated systems would reduce the potential revenue from the sale of the businesses.

Consequently, it was decided to bring all six business units within the reporting unit onto a unified accounting system based on ERP technology. SAP was selected as the software and the decision was taken in 1997 to proceed with the implementation. As the major focus of the programme was unification of the disparate accounting systems and processes of the business units and avoidance of millennium bug-related problems, the system implementation could be described as a 'replacement' as opposed to one that was driven by a 'heavy-benefits' case. This distinction had a major influence on the ultimate assessment of the success of the implementation.

'They had to do something…ongoing operations were at risk and they would have struggled to sell the businesses if they hadn't put new systems in, because of the millennium threat, etc. …'

The organisation had a very ingrained culture – many of the employees had been working in the same relatively unchanging environment for at least 15 years. They were used to doing their tasks one way, and one way only. In terms of the organisation itself, the Finance Department and the Management Accountants within it included some very high calibre individuals who were also (because of the organisational capability of recruiting some of the very best people) very intelligent but (because they had been with the company for so long) they were highly resistant to change in their role or in the manner in which they performed their tasks. They were very accustomed to doing things in a particular way and had very fixed views of how things should be done.

Before the implementation, the reporting unit within BBB was very business function-oriented. Because each business unit was fundamentally a stand-alone company, there was a 'silo' mentality between them and little need for cross-business analysis. Each operating unit was judged on its own merits and, as long as it was meeting its targets, the management of the overall reporting unit saw no need for cross-unit business analysis other than for consolidated reporting.

On a 7-point scale (where 1 = do not match and 7 = match completely) the match between the existing organisation and the process-oriented ERP software was assessed as '3.' Unsurprisingly, this mismatch between organisation culture and the ERP software led to difficulties in the implementation process.

The company faced a number of challenges/decisions from the start:

- The business units were going to shift from virtually unintegrated individual data recording and reporting systems to having one information system, one integrated data recording and reporting system, one way of working and one set of commercial and financial processes common to all of them. There was a lot of resistance across the different business units to the idea that they could all use the same information system and recording and reporting processes.

As an example of the nature of the differences that existed, '*if you are raising a purchase order, there are only so many ways you can raise a purchase order or pay an invoice but [the six business units] used different terminology, etc. The challenge was getting [everyone within the business units] to speak and use common language, particularly around data. That was a major challenge – getting acceptance that it was possible for them all to operate equally effectively using one common system.*'

- The switch from a single functional focus to a process focus meant that boundaries between the functions within each business unit and between business units changed because of the implementation of the ERP system. Individuals within the business units had to understand the impacts of the new system upon the organisation and to accept that while using the previous system they did something one way, using the new system they may need to do something different. They also needed to accept that their roles would possibly, and in some cases, did change.

- Reporting caused enormous problems. The Management Accountants had a whole suite of reports that they produced on spreadsheets or directly from the old legacy systems. They wanted to continue to produce exactly the same reports from the new system, something that would have been extremely difficult with the limited SAP functionality that they had opted to purchase (i.e. no business warehouse). Consequently, it would only have been possible if an enormous investment had been made in developing these bespoke reports.

Given the objectives of the implementation, this (business warehouse) was not considered an appropriate use of resources and so the Management Accountants and the users of the existing reports had to be convinced that it was better to learn to use the new system first, see what reporting capability it had and then discover whether or not they could get-by with the standard SAP reports. A way had to be found to overcome their nervousness – '*I'm not sure we can "go-live" without these reports*' – and persuade them to '*give it a go.*'

- Getting the data ready for the new system was also a major challenge. Agreement across all the business units was needed on all '*how to*' issues – on product codes, on how to structure/build the bills of materials, etc. The legacy data held by each business unit was very specific to that particular unit. Operating the new system meant that all the business units would need to share some elements of their data with the other business units: '*the whole principle of shared data created a massive challenge to traditional thinking, which had to be addressed.*'

- Another significant challenge was establishing an appropriate user-support organisation – how to provide helpdesk and support services. The organisation had to decide the nature of support that would be provided by the more technical

IT department and what would be more appropriately provided by non-IT staff, such as management accounting 'super-users.'

The implementation was championed initially by the CIO and CFO of the reporting unit within BBB and one of the business unit managers was appointed as overall sponsor. The implementation took more than 2 years to complete.

The Management Accountants received generic (i.e. non-company-specific) training in the use of SAP but it was only when the system started to take shape in terms of being aligned to their business and business processes that they really started to use it. It was virtually two-thirds of the way through the implementation that the 20 or so Management Accountants in the six business units all began to recognise the value of the new system. The 'real' training in the use of SAP started at that point. Up until then, the only way to try to convince them of its merits was through description, theory and examples in the generic training sessions.

Despite their ultimately accepting the merits of the new system, more than 5 years after completion of the implementation, some of the Management Accountants continue to ignore some of the facilities within SAP and do much as they did on the old system, providing the same reports as before, produced the way they always did, using spreadsheets: *'I still think management accountants tend to be spreadsheet jockeys – they love their spreadsheets and I don't know how you ever move them away from them completely.'* **There were clear corporate governance and Sarbanes–Oxley implications in this, but they were being ignored.**

One of the six business units was divested during the implementation. However, the SAP implementation continued within it, but as a distinct and separate exercise to the one being done with the remaining business units. At the end of the implementation (1999), five business units were reporting into one reporting organisation. There was little change in the number of Management Accountants within the remaining five business units over the period of the implementation.

Immediately the implementation was completed, BBB switched its attention to divesting the remaining five business units. Within 5 years, all five had been sold to independent companies and the reporting organisation has ceased to exist.

The implementation was viewed as a success: *'Their reason for implementing was because of the threat of the millennium, so it was a replacement system as opposed to one that was driven with a "heavy-benefits" case.'* It faced many challenges but these were overcome and, in the end, it was seen as a success by the major players in the parent group, such as the MD, CIO and CFO, because it successfully met the primary objective: *'it did operate and nothing fell over and the business continued to produce products, invoice customers, etc.'* For the same reasons, it was also considered to have been a success by the Management Accountants in the business units, by the consultants and by the technical implementation partner in BBB.

The role of the Management Accountants

Prior to and during the implementation, there were approximately 20 Management Accountants working in the 6 business units. Although there have been some changes in personnel since the system went live in 1999, the number of Management Accountants has remained much as before. All the Management Accountants were on the project team, some full-time. The involvement of the others increased as it got closer to 'go-live.' While the Managing Director and the CFO were championing the project within the business, the project was mainly driven by one of the Management Accountants: '*[He] was extremely strong. He was really driving this thing as well.*'

Use of the system by the Management Accountants

The ERP system supports the basic role that was previously performed by the Management Accountants. As a result, a very high proportion of the work undertaken by the Management Accountants was impacted upon by the ERP implementation.

However, a lot of analysis and a lot of decision support tasks are still performed outside the ERP system because the functionality that was implemented lacks flexibility in reporting. As a result, the Management Accountants still spend a lot of time taking information from the core transaction system, and putting it into spreadsheets, manipulating it and producing reports. Sometimes they ignore the facilities of the ERP system in order to do so.

Overall, they now have far more information available and now produce both functional and cross-functional analysis and reports.

The changing role of the Management Accountants

During and immediately after the implementation, the Management Accountants were major providers of ongoing support to the new system because they had been so actively involved in the actual implementation. This clearly had an impact on their workload at that time.

The implementation '*really affected the Management Accounting Department.*' They now have far more data available to them and can spend more time on analysis and reporting of the external environment in the form of benchmarking, etc.

The emphasis upon individual activities within the role of the Management Accountants has changed considerably. However, although they should now be much better placed to focus on providing a decision support service to the other business functions rather than acting as providers of traditional data collection and analysis, overall their role has not shifted towards their becoming business partners as a result of the ERP implementation, though they are much more active in supporting decision-making.

The extent to which the new system has had an impact on the role of Management Accountants was described as follows.

The scores relate to the question: 'On a scale from 1 to 7 (1: very much reduced to 7: very much increased).'

(a)	Time spent on data collection 'It has gone down.'	Score = 2
(b)	Time spent on data analysis 'Increased.'	Score = 5
(c)	Involvement in business decision-making 'Increased a lot.'	Score = 6
(d)	Focus on internal reporting, for example performance measurement and control issues 'No.'	Score = 4
(e)	Focus on external environment (e.g. benchmarking)	Score = 5

'I don't think it has necessarily increased because of the ERP system. It has probably increased because of the market [changes in the market] that the business is in [but, taking these other factors out of the equation,] it has changed slightly [to 5].'

The following summarises the response to the questions listed below:

(a) *To what extent are traditional analysis performed that focus on past operating results compared to decision support type of analysis that have a forward-looking focus?*

'The decision support is 60–70% of the time as opposed to the other way around [previously] (30–40%).'

(b) *Are the Management Accountants performing cross-functional analysis compared to domain specific analysis?*

'Yes, probably more than they were, although I think they probably still do quite a lot of analysis within the functional silos... [cross-functional analysis] won't replace the [domain specific analysis]... but the difference now is that there is the ability to see, to look at "end to end" business processes across the business and in more depth than previously.'

(c) *Given that it takes less time to get the data, what are the Management Accountants doing with the extra time?*

'Within the organisation, many people have always worked very long hours and despite the introduction of the ERP system they still do [work long hours]. I guess the more information they have available the more analysis is possible.'

I do believe there is a need to sometimes challenge them and say, 'How much of it adds real value and therefore how much of it is really necessary?'

'But I also suspect something else is contributing to the work load and that is .... they have been under pressure as an organisation in terms of cost reduction and efficiency, therefore probably what has happened is they just haven't recruited additional people... they are probably just doing less of some things and more of others with the same number of people.'

(d) *Has the way they communicate with the other people in the organisation changed?*

'I think [in the case of] the [Operating unit] that I know most about since the divestment... if you look at the [chief management accountant] and the people that work for him, I think he has become much more immersed in the business than he ever was... he used to be somebody who was slightly on a limb whereas now he is an integral part of the management group.'

(e) *Would the communication that he had with other managers in other functions within the business, have tended to be formal or informal?*

'The organisation has been successful for many years with a very strong informal communication structure, which I think is still very strong. Although I suspect following divestment to a US company the level of formal communications will have increased.'

(f) *Has job satisfaction altered for the Management Accountants?*

'I would imagine yes.'

(g) *How have the Management Accountants contributed to the success of the new system?*

'Tremendous – it would not have happened if it weren't for them.'

The approach adopted to bring the Management Accountants on board

The following summarises the response by the Management Consultant to the questions listed below:

(a) *How did the Management Accountants end up as the drivers of the new system?*

'We put an enormous amount of effort into ensuring appropriate involvement not only from the management accountants but also from other business representatives. Our approach had to be insistent, tenacious and enduring to ensure effective participation of the broader business community with the project team. I admit at times it felt like we were having to drag some people to the table "kicking and screaming."'

'At the same time, we had to be supportive and make sure that we did whatever we could to ease the burden on them. We always tried to ask for their help rather than demand their input and sometimes played to their egos by claiming that things simply could not progress forward without their support. And it was difficult, because at the time from an accounting viewpoint, they had far too much work on and they were effectively trying to fit the demands of the system implementation into their spare time. Over time, things became much easier as the rapport and understanding between us increased and also as they started to see the necessity and benefit of their contribution.'

'But it had to be... relentless. You couldn't... "let them off the hook" i.e. you couldn't get them involved one week and then let them not participate for two months, you had to find ways to maintain their involvement throughout. Although it is important to recognise that their time involvement did vary depending on the stage of implementation with an obvious overall increase as the programme progressed towards go-live.'

(b) *Did you work with all of them or just with some of them?*

'Just with some of them. We worked closely with at least one representative of each business unit, who in turn then worked with their broader business community.'

(c) *Did you do this with any other functional group within the company?*

'Yes. Although finance had a very high profile we also had to ensure that the other business functions, e.g. Sales and distribution, procurement, manufacturing, etc. were also adequately represented and involved. We also used cross-functional workshop type events to bring people from different parts of the organisation together to understand the "end to end" integrated business processes that the ERP system introduced.'

(d) *Did the Management Accountants get any training in the use of SAP while you were doing this?*

'Yes, they did. I think most of them found the SAP training that they received in the early stages not particularly useful because it was generally too generic and theoretical. It was only when they could experience the functionality in the context of their actual business unit and business processes that it really meant anything.'

'Because of the high profile of the finance community during the implementation and because of the relatively small number of people, the majority of the accounting staff had the opportunity to gain hands-on experience of the new system during the different phases of the implementation. This ultimately meant that a lot of the finance training was delivered much more informally, i.e. as opposed to formal classroom training required for the other business functions.'

(e) *Did they get any advice or instruction in a formal sense in what an ERP system is?*
'Yes, at the beginning of the program there were various educational events and demonstrations designed to introduce the concept of ERP and the capabilities of ERP and what it can do and what it can't do. I think some people found it quite difficult to absorb as it was quite theoretical and not necessarily delivered in the context of their business. I also think it created some unrealistic expectations for some people, particularly in terms of reporting flexibility and capability.'

Recommendations for Management Accountants

The following summarises the responses to the questions (listed below) about recommendations for Management Accountants involved in the implementation and use of ERP systems.

(a) *What skills would you recommend for Management Accountants that have recently implemented ERP systems?*
- broaden their thinking and become more multidimensional
- educator skills
- analytical skills
- numeracy skills
- technical skills
- interpersonal skills (because they need to be able to communicate
- ability to work effectively with non-accountants
- patience – SAP can be difficult to use at first
- ability to prioritise – work management
- business partnering
- to be focused – it is easy to be distracted

'To me, **the skills**... however you define skills, competencies, whatever... **the critical ones that I would be looking for are more behavioural, interpersonal, etc** ... I would tend to take it as read that if somebody was a qualified Management Accountant... they'd have appropriate analytical, numeracy, etc. skills.'

'[They are] going to be working in an Accounting Department but [they are] going to be involved in everything... I have met and worked with lots of accountants that noticed that, in reality, often the less successful ones are those with the poorest interpersonal skills. Unfortunately when organisations recruit accountants they focus on qualifications and technical experience and rarely focus on *interpersonal or behavioural skills. I feel very strongly that an accountant's ability to relate and work effectively with non-accountants and other functional specialists is imperative especially in an ERP environment where all the systems and processes are integrated and therefore interdependant.'*

'*[Traditionally], accountants have worked with accountants, using standalone legacy financial systems and all speaking a common language, which is often unintelligible to non-accountants. Whereas, in an ERP environment, accountants need to work much more closely with other business functions within the organisation, using shared integrated systems and speaking a common business language – not an easy transition for some to make.*'

(b) *What is 'best practice' for a Management Accountant working with this type of system?*
- Accountants should stop behaving as 'servants' and start educating and encouraging other functional staff to use the system to do their own analysis. A good example is overhead analysis.
- They should manage by exception rather than analysing minutiae and should focus on trends rather than absolutes.
- They should work in closely and partnership with the other business functions, rather than as the 'arms length gatekeeper.'
- They should focus on providing support rather than control and providing information rather than data.

(c) *What guidance would you provide for Management Accountants in organisations that have recently implemented ERP systems?*
- Expect and plan for a productivity dip in the first 2 or 3 months (learning curve).
- Challenge traditional reporting.
- Don't assume the integrity of migrated data.
- Stick with it, keep an open mind, be patient.

(d) *How should Management Accountants use ERP systems?*
- To empower others.
- To improve data integrity.
- To simplify processes and automate elements of internal control.
- As a source of information, not as a source of data, that is as an MIS, not as a data repository.

Summary

In BBB, after a very slow start, the Management Accountants became major drivers of the implementation. The ERP system fulfils the basic role that was previously performed by the Management Accountants, and has empowered them to shift their role from data collectors towards a greater emphasis upon data analysis, reporting of the external environment in the form of benchmarking, etc. and acting as Business Accountants supporting decision-making.

Whether individual Management Accountants have made this shift in their role has been very much a matter of personal choice. Some have preferred to continue as before, even to the extent of ignoring some of the facilities of the ERP system and using spreadsheets to produce bespoke reports similar to those they produced under the previous legacy system.

In this ERP environment, it is recommended that beyond the normal accounting and technical skills, Management Accountants must possess good communication and interpersonal skills and have the ability to work with non-accountants. In addition, good numeracy and analytical skills, good work management skills and an ability to focus are seen as important attributes to possess.

One final comment was made by the interviewee. It concerned post-implementation and, in this case, the absence of any benefits-tracking system from the implementation. She felt that as it was a replacement project rather than a benefit-driven one, there was not the perceived need for a tracking system of this type – the benefits were clear without one. However, she felt that in any benefits-driven implementation, having a benefits-tracking system was essential: *'management accountants [should] insist [upon having] and driving [the development] of... benefit-tracking processes... So, if they say this system is going to deliver [say] £20 million of benefits, we would expect that to be broken down [with] clearly defined accountabilities [relating to individual] input [to the project so] that you can... [then] put in a sophisticated benefit tracking system.'*

Case C

This organisation (referred to as CCC) is a very large UK-based international audio and telecommunications production and distribution company. A Senior Executive (finance) described the case of the ERP system implementation across the organisation. All quotes are from the Senior Executive.

Background

In 2000, CCC completed implementation of various modules of SAP, including all the finance modules: Sales Ledger, Purchase Ledger, General Ledger, Fixed Assets, the whole suite from that perspective. Only some of the non-finance modules were implemented.

The implementation of SAP at CCC was part of a two-part change strategy aimed at reducing costs to the organisation. Firstly, all CCC's financial transaction processing was outsourced, and then SAP was implemented across CCC.

In 1996, CCC benchmarked itself with external organisations. This led to a conclusion that CCC's finance costs were at least 2–3 times more expensive than they should have been for an organisation of its size and complexity. There was obvious duplication across the organisation – for example, 36 different general ledger systems were in use across CCC and all the different divisions of CCC had their own small finance teams, including transaction processing.

To address the issues highlighted by the benchmarking exercise, transaction processing was centralised within CCC for 1 year. Then, in 1997, CCC entered into a contract with a joint venture between a 'big-4' accounting firm and a top-100 Fortune 500 consultancy company specialising in business and technology solutions to improve business performance.

The contract was in two parts. Firstly, transaction processing was outsourced to the joint venture and all those employed on transaction processing within CCC were transferred into the new organisation.

Secondly, in order to streamline the business information system and eliminate duplication, CCC decided (with the assistance of the joint venture) to switch to an SAP-based system that would not only be implemented across the entire organisation but also used in the same way, irrespective of where in the organisation it was being used. That is, from the outset, bespoke items, such as specially written reports were replaced by generic, organisation-wide practices.

The implementation team comprised of consultants from the joint venture and CCC staff. At its height, there were between 70 and 80 CCC employees working on the implementation team. There were approximately 6000 users on the initial implementation, though this has been reduced to around 4000 as it became clearer who would actually use the system.

Implementation of SAP took approximately 3 years. Rollout was in three phases. Firstly, a pilot implementation was done in one of the geographical divisions of CCC (which was, in effect, a mini-version of CCC). Then, in November 1999, SAP was rolled-out into half of the other divisions. The third phase occurred at the start of April 2000, when SAP was rolled-out into the rest of CCC. (This latter date was carefully selected in order to have the new system implemented across the organisation at the start of its 2000/2001 financial year, thus avoiding any problems arising from converting from one accounting system to another mid-financial year.)

Savings arose from the outsourcing of transaction processing and other efficiency savings within CCC (e.g. the number of Management Accountants was reduced by outsourcing) but by far the greatest contributor to annual cost savings of about £17.5 million a year since implementation is the SAP system, and *'that is after allowing for the cost of SAP.'* In achieving cost savings of this magnitude, the initial targeted savings were met; and, because the initial targeted savings were of this level, the implementation project consistently received strong backing from the very top of the organisation.

It was about 18 months after rollout that people began to see the benefits of the system. By that time, a full year's business cycle had been completed. The budget had been done, a financial year-end had been completed and a lot of initial teething problems had been addressed.

The Management Accountants were among the first to feel the benefits of the implementation.

'I think SAP is like a lot of other systems. Part of the problem is that when you implement these systems, the pain is felt in one place and the gains felt somewhere else. So the Management Accountants felt the gain quite early on in the life cycle whereas the poor [people] sitting at the sharp end having to raise purchase orders, and all that kind of stuff, they [were] feeling the pain and they [didn't] really see the benefits... of the system because they [were] much further up the value chain. But I think that is the same with all big systems implementations.'

The project had two key champions. The one whose commitment was essential in the early stages was the CEO, who took up his role just as the final 'go:no-go' decision was about to be made. Traditionally, within CCC, finance has been seen as a support function rather than one that leads change. If the Chief Executive had not championed the project, it would have been very difficult for the finance function to have convinced the key players in the organisation that going through such enormous change would be beneficial to them.

'*He had to be convinced that it was the right thing to do. But once he had been convinced that is was, he was very vocal in support of [it,] which was absolutely critical in terms of rolling it out... We needed [the CEO] as a leader of the [key players] to be the person saying, "Yes, we should be doing this kind of thing."*'

The visionary and other key champion behind the project was the current Chief Operating Officer (COO) of CCC. Once the Chief Executive had given his backing to the project and established commitment throughout the organisation, even had he then left the company, the COO would have been able to drive the project to completion.

The Senior Executive (finance) viewed SAP as business function-orientated and CCC as business process orientated when the project started. Although there has been some movement towards bringing the orientation of CCC closer to that of SAP, the match between SAP and the organisational structure of CCC is now only about 4 on a scale of 1–7, where 1 is no match and 7 a perfect match.

'**It is getting closer but it matches more now [September 2004] than it did at the time [1997], but I would not describe them as completely aligned.**'

The project is considered to have been a success. Quite apart from the financial benefits, success can also be seen in:

- Halving of the time taken to do monthly reporting to the Board level, from 18 to 19 days down to 9 days – a significant saving in terms of the time it takes to close the accounts.
- Vastly improved reporting as a result of greatly improved visibility of and access to information – '*even the most senior managers who have very little contact with SAP will say that "The thing that SAP has given me is huge visibility of costs so that you can run reports on costs, you can control projects better."*'
- The ability to build on the base that SAP has provided, bringing in information from other sources in a way that could not have been achieved before.
- Budgetary control has improved because there is now more time available for analysis and more exception reporting being done.
- More is being done with less people.
- The basic level of financial controls has improved to the point that for the last 2 years, the external auditors have had no major issues with anything in the organisation.

Although outsourcing transaction processing saved significant amounts of money, the transaction processes that were outsourced to the joint venture were poor – '*they were not very slick and there were lots of problems with them.*' The design of these processes resulted in a split system, part of which was in CCC and part of which was outside CCC. Unfortunately, SAP was rolled-out before the transaction processing problems were dealt with. It then took a long time to unpick some of the problems that arose from the inefficient design of the transaction processing system.

'We should have done more re-engineering before we actually did the implementation rather than afterwards. With hindsight, the inappropriateness of the transaction processes should have been addressed before SAP was rolled out.'

'But, a) we wanted to get the money out of the system, and b) you talk to other organisations... at the end of the day, we just had to force SAP into the organisation and then sort the issues out afterwards. If we hadn't stuck to our guns and said "we are going to do this", the business would have thought of millions, hundreds of reasons why we shouldn't go with SAP.'

'Culturally, it was about centralisation, about standardisation and CCC at that time was an organisation that wasn't into centralized decision making or that kind of thing. And therefore we really just had to force the issue and hold our nerve. But it meant that we then had to do some things [afterwards] that, in retrospect, would have been best done [beforehand].'

The level of success of the SAP implementation at CCC was felt to be due to the following:

(a) Strong championing of the implementation at the highest level in the organisation.
(b) Standardisation wherever possible.
(c) Use of vanilla SAP unless it was clearly better to make bespoke adjustments to the system.
(d) Achievement of buy-in to the system across the organisation.
(e) The ability to build on the base that SAP has provided, bringing in information from other sources in a way that could not have been achieved before, including the impending roll-out of a business data warehouse. (A utility that sits across the top of SAP which enables manipulation of large volumes of data both from within and outside of SAP).

The role of the Management Accountants

Although job satisfaction and staff turnover among Management Accountants has remained fairly constant, **the number of Management Accountants has been reduced by approximately one-third since SAP was implemented**. In effect, they are doing more with less.

Use of the system by the Management Accountants

CCC tried to encourage as much use of SAP as possible. The management reporting timetable was redesigned so that it encourages use of the system by making it easier to do work on-system, rather than off-system. At first, a lot of Monthly Management Reporting was done off-system (the reports that went to local Boards and Divisional teams were done off-system) but for 18 months from early 2003, a team was set up that went round each division rolling out report packs that come straight off the system so that only commentaries and some non-financial information have to be added outside SAP in order to get what they want.

Now, approximately 25–30% of the work of the Management Accountants is done away from SAP. Some still prepare their budgets on Excel spreadsheets and then enter the data into SAP; and some management reporting is still prepared off-system; but this 25–30% also includes all the other things that they do as well, such as discussions with non-finance staff and managers. Clearly, there are Sarbanes–Oxley implications in this off-system work and the organisation is looking at 'how to get rid of [these] bespoke aspects of the system.'

The changing role of the Management Accountants

The role of the Management Accountants has changed since the implementation of SAP they spend far less time preparing their monthly management accounts and their monthly reports – 9 days instead of 18 or 19. As a result, they now have much more time to look at business support, actually analysing what the accounts are telling them, and working with the business helping it make the right decisions based on that information, and at a lower level than before.

They are also able to do far more monitoring of variances than under the previous system and can make sure that big projects stay within their budget. In addition, as many things are now centralised, they can drive through things they previously had little involvement in, such as changes in procurement policies.

The extent to which the new system had an impact on the role of Management Accountants was described by the Senior Executive (finance).

The scores relate to the question: 'On a scale from 1 to 7 (1: very much reduced to 7: very much increased).'

(a) *Time spent on data collection* 'It has gone down.'	Score = 1
(b) *Time spent on data analysis* 'The analysis has gone up.'	Score = 6

(c) *Involvement in business decision-making* | **Score = 7**

'It has gone up a lot.'

(d) *Focus on internal reporting, for example performance measurement and control issues* | **Score = 6**

'That has gone up slightly.'

(e) *Focus on external environment (e.g. benchmarking)* | **Score = 7**

'That has gone up... a lot.'

The following summarises the responses to the questions listed below:

(a) *To what extent is the analysis that they undertake now looking into the future as opposed to looking at the past?*

'It is about 60% future and 40% historical.[Previously] it would have been the other way [round] because there was much less trust in the numbers before we had SAP.'

(b) *What is the balance between Management Accountants' activity on cross-functional analysis compared to domain specific analysis?*

'There is so much more cross-functional stuff now. That was one of our frustrations with the old system particularly when you had 36 General Ledger [systems] and you could hardly do anything across the whole [organisation], or even across your divisions in some instances. We only had 7 divisions and we had 36 General Ledgers. The sub-divisions didn't even have the same General Ledgers or bits of it.'

(c) *Given that it takes less time to get the data, what are the Management Accountants doing with the extra time?*

'Supporting the business and decision making... we would say now that things like our budgeting are much better and our forecasting are much better. To give you an example, 3 years ago we didn't really do any serious cash forecasting. As a result of which, it was always dire – tens and tens of millions out... Fortunately, it was always better than we said it was going to be. But now, divisions are fantastic at doing cash forecasting – of necessity to a large extent – **so that is what they are concentrating their time with. More forward-looking and on things we really didn't do a lot of work on previously.**'

(d) *Has the way they communicate with the other people in the organisation changed?*

'I don't think it has changed very much. It tends to be informal because CCC is quite an informal organisation culturally. [We] are not greatly into formality in any way, shape, or form.'

(e) *Has job satisfaction altered for the Management Accountants?*
'No... they do more but... they enjoyed their jobs before and they enjoy them now, so I wouldn't think it [has changed] that much really.'

(f) *How have the Management Accountants contributed to the success of the new system?*
'Undoubtedly they did. They were realistic about [two things]: we [had] (a) some bespoke work done on SAP and we have (b) done changes to processes as a result of SAP. The management accountants were quite good at both promoting the need for change where they said the way the vanilla SAP did it was unworkable and we need to change this. But, at the same time, they were quite good at saying, "Well, actually, we could change our processes to fit in with that."'

'And I think **they were invaluable on getting the business to accept the changes** because that was our big problem – getting non-finance people [to buy into] it. The Management Accountants were the people closest to the non-finance [people] and they... worked with non-finance staff to get it... implemented.'

The approach adopted to bring the Management Accountants on board

Management Accountants were involved throughout the project. The project team included about 20 Management Accountants not all of whom were working purely on management accounting aspects of the project – some were part of the implementation project. In addition, CCC took the view that involving the Management Accountants in the implementation was crucial. As a result, between 30 and 40 other Management Accountants who were not, themselves, on the project team were involved in the implementation in some way from the business perspective.

The changing role of the Management Accountant in successful/unsuccessful implementations

The Senior Executive (finance) of CCC felt that the degree of success achieved in an ERP implementation does make a difference to the changes that it brings to the role of the Management Accountant. For example, in less successful implementations, more time would be spent 'fire-fighting' and trying to make the best of a bad job. In contrast, when the implementation is successful, the Management Accountant can spend much more time working on how to further improve the system.

'An awful lot of [management accounting] time...is [now] focussed on how we get even more costs out and it is very forward looking: it's how we get more costs out, it is how we get the best reporting out of Business Warehouse, how we get rid *of the bespoke aspects of the system so we go back to more vanilla systems. So, it is quite a positive approach that we've got because we have been successful and I think that does make quite a difference.'*

Recommendations for Management Accountants

The following summarises the responses to the questions (listed below) about recommendations for Management Accountants involved in the implementation and use of ERP systems.

(a) *What skills would you recommend for Management Accountants that have recently implemented ERP systems?*

The Senior Executive (finance) felt that the suite of basic skills Management Accountants need in an ERP environment was pretty much the same as in a traditional environment but that some of the emphasis might be a bit different. The following were seen as essential skills:
- Interpersonal skills

    'More... interpersonal skills than... previously. That would be the big change, to make sure that people could work with the business.'
- analytical skills
- decision-making ability
- ability to prioritise
- planning skills – time management, both short-term and long-term

'There is a danger when you have a new system that there is so much information (and one of the things that I have said is good about our SAP implementation is the fact that you can get loads more information out) they need the analysis ability but, together with that, they need the decision-making ability to decide what is important and what isn't important; because I think that there [is] a danger to start with that you could just get overwhelmed with the [amount of] data coming at you and they [have] to be able to prioritise what [is] the stuff we really [need] to look at and what we [don't] need to look at. The other thing I think they [need is] really good planning skills, both day-to-day planning skills and also turning those into the ability to do longer term budgeting and forecasting.'

'We say everything has to be to us by the end of working day 6. Now it is up to them... there is some remit for them to decide how long they spend doing their actuals and how long they spend doing their forecasting and they've had to be able to manage that process so at least, come day 6, they can have good actuals and good forecasts in the system. And they have some kind of leeway to do that.'

- influence and persuasion skills

    '***They needed to have influencing and persuading skills*** *and this goes back to what I just said about working with local non-finance people: the [management accountants] have to be able to convince them that it [is] a good system and that it [is] worth engaging with [it].*'
- Leadership skills

    '***They had to [provide] leadership****, particularly among their own finance… local finance teams, in terms of taking them with them. The time management stuff I talked about… having made the decision about how they were going to allocate and do things, they then have to bring their own teams with them.*'
- Software skills
- IT Skills

    '*They probably need slightly less now. It is difficult with SAP because it is such a non-intuitive system that you have to have some kind of level of [these] skills. But on the other hand… as part of rolling out SAP… we centralised a lot of the reporting in terms of… the writing of reports… so there is a lot less involvement locally with actually setting up reports. You might run them but, actually, they are off a central suite of reports. So you need to have less IT skills I think from that.*'

    '*And now we are rolling out Business Warehouse [and] one thing I like about [it] is they can do more tailored reporting. But, actually, we are keeping the skills to actually develop Business Warehouse reports very localised so that we have designated experts rather than everybody becoming a… Business Warehouse report writing [expert].*'

    '*From an IT perspective, in some senses we've de-skilled them but, on the other hand, you have to first [have the skills to] cope with SAP, which is not the easiest system in the world.*'

(b) What is 'best practice' for a Management Accountant working with this type of system?

- Standardisation

    '*I think the worst thing that they can [do is to try] to de-standardize things… we have tried to standardize across the [organisation] and I think that one of the worst things that they can do is say "Well, actually…" This is probably the same in every other organisation but particularly in CCC, everybody thinks that they are special, their division is special and therefore they should be doing it differently. I think that is the worst sin you can commit because unless you have really got a genuine reason – and I think there are very few – **you should be going for the standardized approach as much as possible**.*'

(c) What guidance would you provide for Management Accountants in organisations that have recently implemented ERP systems?

- Change working practices to work with the software unless there is a good reason for not doing so.

(d) *How should Management Accountants use ERP systems?*
- Don't get carried away with what the system can do – make it work for you by producing the information you need, not the other way around.

'It is a fantastic system and it does fantastic things for us but if we don't get it to produce the right management information then it is not... any good for us... you don't want to be in a situation where the system has taken over. Just because you have this fantastic piece of software that you have rolled out everywhere... at the end of the day, you have to be able to stand back and say "What do I actually want out of the system?" before you start touching the system, otherwise you are not really gaining the benefits from it.'

Summary

In CCC, the Management Accountants were heavily involved in the implementation. The ERP system has empowered them to spend more time working with the business and has enabled them to undertake greater amounts of data analysis which, in turn, has led to greatly improved budgetary control and forecasting throughout the organisation.

Some of the Management Accountants – those with the better interpersonal skills – made the change to having a greater involvement with the business. Some were less successful in adapting their role in this way to fit the new SAP environment.

The organisation has become far more standardised and has increased centralisation of activities, such as procurement. This would not have been possible under the previous system. One consequence of this is that more cross-functional analysis is being done than previously, thus providing an increased awareness of relative performance across the organisation.

In this ERP environment, it is recommended that beyond the normal accounting and technical skills, Management Accountants should possess greater interpersonal skills than in a non-ERP environment and have the ability to work with non-accountants. All other skills typically required of a Management Accountant working in a traditional environment continue to be essential, though the degree of importance they have in the role may be greater or less in an ERP environment.

Case D

DDD is a listed company in the global food services and beverage industry. A Senior Executive (finance) describes the case of the ERP system implementation. All quoted comments are from this Senior Executive.

Background

DDD has a distribution network in over 50 countries, and an international franchise business that comprises over 10,000 outlets. About one-third of their business is in Europe, one-half in North America and the remainder in Latin America and Asia.

DDD is in the process of rolling out an end-to-end SAP R/3 implementation. The selection and impetus for the SAP system originated in one of the European offices and was subsequently embraced for all of Europe, the UK and North America (for part of the business). The project was initially championed mostly from an IT perspective and did not have sufficient business focus. In addition, the project had a country focus, and was not directly scalable up to a complete company level. The initial implementation, a 'big bang', was temporarily stopped for a variety of reasons, and was not viewed as a success (it was scored a 2 out of 7, with 7 representing very successful). The implementation focused on the most difficult parts (commercial interfaces with complex non-standard trade terms, etc.), rather than on getting the 'quick wins.' Additionally, the invoicing system that was implemented in one country did not work, and no back-up system existed.

DDD originally tried to fit SAP around the existing business practices rather than identifying the appropriate business processes and then implementing SAP. This resulted in a mismatch between the process-oriented ERP system and the function-oriented business structure. An additional complication was the lack of discipline in some areas to ensure that SAP would be used from the lowest level (e.g. raising purchase orders) to the highest level (e.g. corporate and statutory accounts). DDD believed that the problems were more related to the lower level processes as the corporate financial reporting system was providing timely information.

When the implementation was halted, a decision was then made to simplify the current business practices so they would better match the way that SAP processes the transactions. About 2 years have been spent on retrenching with about 30% of the transactions going through SAP. DDD expects that they will need to spend at least another 2 years to get 70–80% of their major locations in the UK and Europe onto SAP. Currently, the match between the process-oriented ERP system and the function-oriented business structure is about 3 on a scale of 1–7, where 1 is no match and 7 a perfect match.

In order to rescue the project, the financial group quietly continued to work on rebuilding the credibility of the system, '…going underground, keeping quiet and getting it working and then emerging and being able to do stuff we could never do before.'

Rather than conducting a full-blown business process re-engineering engagement, the financial group conducted 'stealth reengineering.' Once they were able to get a process to work well in a shared service centre, they would shut down that function in other locations and transfer it to the shared service centre. Finance is viewed as having done things well; they are much more efficient than before, for example requiring one person to look after statutory accounts compared to five people before.

The company is now focused on defining data standards that will be applied to the entire organisation. The current Chart of Accounts has over 3700 accounts across multiple countries, but was not designed to aggregate the information by account on a company level (versus country level). This will provide input to the data warehouse that is under construction. The new financial management system based upon the data warehouse is very scalable throughout the company.

The improved ERP system provides enhancements in data quality and speed of reporting. '…we have a bit more confidence in the data we have got and we can get it out faster. If you were to ask me what my main job was here, it's to guide this company onto its expectations with no surprises. And we couldn't do that with what I inherited. Significant progress has now been achieved.'

The role of the Management Accountants

There were no Management Accountants involved in the initial design of the financial portion of the system. There were a number of financial staff involved, but they did not have the appropriate perspective to really identify what the processes should do and how to simplify the process. Now, for the redesign of the processes several of DDD's most capable Management Accountants are involved.

Use of the system by the Management Accountants

The ERP system has greatly simplified all of the inter-company reporting, that in the past was very complex. At the present time, 80% of the Management Accountants' effort is spent generating numbers and checking that the numbers are correct. Once everything is moved onto SAP and the data warehouse, DDD expects that there will be a reduction from 55 to 33 Management Accountants.

The changing role of the Management Accountants

The role of the Management Accountant is changing at DDD. The comment was made that '... *I need some more people with business and analytical nous, more MBA type Management Accountants.*' This was in comparison to the 'traditional' report generating management accountant. There is the need for analysts who focus on financial models and the implications of the outputs of those models. Too much of the management accountant's time is spent on reporting and not enough on analysis '...*today, we have Management Accountants all around the world generating a P&L Report which [are] all slightly different using slightly different conventions. All that disappears when we go live [with a data warehouse and standardised data].*'

The Management Accountant must become a business partner, '...*you want the people who know the business, who can work with the business leaders, the business people and make the finances work for them whether it be helping them do things, whether it be helping them control things, or whether or most importantly, challenging them to say, "Wait a minute, we are spending a £1 million on this. Where is the payback? How does this economic model work? Are there better options? What critical things do we have to make sure goes right so we achieve our objectives". So it is very much the partnership piece with the key decision makers.*' The Management Accountants who will continue on at DDD will need to be proactive business partners, not just report generators.

DDD is developing various financial models that use the historic data to generate forward-looking analyses. This was not possible prior to the improved ERP system and data warehouse and financial modelling system that has recently been implemented. This is helping expedite changes in the role of the Management Accountant, from an emphasis on past-looking to forward-looking data. In the past, the Management Accountant spent about 75% of the time on past-looking data. The ratio has been reduced to about 55% past-looking data and the objective is to move to even more forward-looking data.

The extent to which the new system has had an impact on the role of Management Accountants on the following functions was described as follows:

The scores relate to the question: 'On a scale from 1 to 7 (1: very much reduced to 7: very much increased).'

(a)	Time spent on data collection	Score = 3
(b)	Time spent on data analysis	Score = 5
(c)	Involvement in business decision-making	Score = 4

(d) *Focus on internal reporting, for example, performance measurement and control issues*	Score = 7
(e) *Focus on external environment (e.g. benchmarking)*	Score = 3

The following summarises the response to the questions listed below:

(a) *To what extent are traditional analysis performed that focus on past operating results compared to decision support type of analysis that have a forward-looking focus?*

There is a push to get the Management Accountants to provide more forward-looking, decision support type of analysis, compared to classic spreadsheet and graphics preparation.

'… *unfortunately too many people are spending time behind computer screens tarting-up reports. One of the classic examples is the Executive Report which we produce every month. The archetype Management Accountant would be there and say, "We have the data in ok." And I would then ask them, "What have you been doing?" "We have been tarting-up the tables. I would like to add a graph." And I would challenge, "What insight is it you want to get across? What are your main points?" And they would then write a commentary that simply describes the standard graph. And then I would move to coaching mode and say, "No guys look at the data, Think through what this means for the business. What is good, bad, opportunity or risk? Is there anything unexpected?* **What does it mean looking forward for us to achieve our targets?** *OK, now design a graphic and commentary that communicates the main points." Some of the guys are getting it – but unfortunately not all. That is the sort of shift we have got to have. There is a lot of comfort blanket in reporting and software, it is quite difficult to be out there and exposed through making your own views clear at the decision support end.*'

(b) *Are the Management Accountants performing cross-functional analysis compared to domain specific analysis?*

The biggest advantage that occurred as a result of the SAP project was the creation of a data warehouse using a different software application (Hyperion). The Hyperion application is able to perform analyses based upon a financial model of the company that was not possible only with SAP. The Hyperion tool allows for significant cross-functional analysis than was done before. DDD considers this to be a significant step forward in their capabilities, but also laments that this is where DDD should have been before. Efforts to improve cross-functional analysis are also being pursued beyond the ERP.

(c) *Since less time is needed for data capture and less time is spent generating routine reports for managers, what are the Management Accountants doing with the extra time?*

The objective is to use the extra time for performing more 'what next' analysis. This is to move the business to where it needs to be from both a financial and business strategy perspective. This also includes going beyond financial analysis to controls, and whether the business is getting where it needs to be, including the metrics to measure the controls.

(d) *Have the communication skills of the Management Accountants become more significant and important than they were before?*

To be an effective business partner, the Management Accountant needs to master communication both to and from the decision-makers they support. They need to be prepared to use the necessary art of persuasion – understanding how their executives make their decisions and adapt accordingly. Sometimes this may not be straightforward.

'For example, I recall a case when a Director appeared to want to see the same data but in three different ways. I had to coach the management accountant concerned to kerb his frustration and represent the data, and communicate what it meant each time (not surprisingly the same main conclusions). In the end the Director made the call and was happy with the support he got. The point is, a manager will not always make a decision based simply on a report, but may ask around and gather enough information until they have been through the issues from all angles. It was a big call and our job was to support him making it.'

Timing is another issue. Executives ask their questions or ask for analysis at the most inconvenient times or with impossible lead times. However, the Management Accountant must recognise that a window of opportunity will exist when '… we are going to get their attention on a particular subject and you have to be able to hit the buttons **for what they are looking for at that time**. You can have some fantastic insight but if you are not going to present it in the right form at the right time, then it is wasted.'

'…what I am also looking for from my people, are people who can actually come up with something that is not immediately obvious in the information or data. Business acumen, talent, etc.'

(e) *Has the formal or informal communication structure involving the Management Accountants changed as a result of the new system implementation?*

The formal approach is producing a report, give it to a manager and then disappear until the manager calls back. The informal approach has the Management Accountant call on the manager, tell the manager that there is a problem and go through the analysis with the manager. It is acceptable if the manager does not act immediately on the issue. The Management Accountant is alerting the manager, and after the manager has the opportunity to investigate it, the manager will call the Management Accountant back. 'As long as there is genuine follow up it is ok. Of course if there is no action and the issue is important, the issue will get picked up in the financial roll up of progress in the Division. The key point is transparency throughout. So, I think on the whole, we tend to the more informal approach but the key point is recognising the objective is to make good decisions and it is not just about producing an impressive report.'

(f) *How satisfied were the Management Accountants, both prior to and post the new system implementation?*

There has been some self-selection on the part of some Management Accountants to leave the company. On a personal level, the new job tasks and the ERP implementation itself are very hard work. The Management Accountants agree that the ERP system is the appropriate solution. However, when asked about job satisfaction, they say that the implementation and new way of doing things is just too much hard work.

There has been attrition during the period of raising the immediate game and implementing a longer-term solution. Several Management Accountants have left because they were just tired, that they just had enough. That said, the newcomers think that everything is fine. The wear and tear and dynamics of this level of change should not be underestimated.

(g) *How have the Management Accountants contributed to the success of the new system?*

The Management Accountants are contributing to the incremental success of the ERP system. **You need to have the right people involved, and this most definitely includes the Management Accountants.** In order to successfully implement an ERP system you need people who can understand the business central to the implementation, not someone from the outside.

The changing role of the Management Accountant in successful/unsuccessful implementations

Management Accountants need to change from only being producers of reports. They need to be able to look at a report and identify those key items that are important and present the information in such a way that senior people will be motivated to notice, consider and act. **In a successful ERP system implementation, the Business Partner role is going to be a lot easier for the Management Accountant to perform** than with an unsuccessful one, where they will remain bogged down in data verification.

Recommendations for Management Accountants

The following summarises the responses to the questions (listed below) about recommendations for Management Accountants involved in the implementation and use of ERP systems.

(a) *What skills would you recommend for Management Accountants that have recently implemented ERP systems?*
- A combination of being able to get the big picture for the company concerned and synthesise hypotheses and opportunities.
- Be able to relate to and understand the business (and create a financial/economic model of the business to analyse and exploit). The best ones will reach well beyond finance data and bring in multifunctional and outside data to their analysis.
- Partnership/close relationship role with managers (without going 'native').
- Support the making of big decisions, influencing managers onto the right ground.
- Communication skills to explain the analysis to allow the manager to understand the issue and take appropriate action.
- The traditional number crunching skills are less important since the ERP system can produce those numbers; the Management Accountant needs to produce insights.
- Of course you need a first class financial accountant and FSC administrator to turn the handle on the ERP machine fast, efficiently and cost effectively.

With the new system, communication skills are extremely important. 'I have had some pretty tough calls recently because I have got an executive team of people who, on a professional level, are great, I mean, they can give me an outstanding technical brief on, for example, IFRS or implementing Sarbanes–Oxley but the feedback from the business people is that they do not relate or are not understood and therefore not engaged by them. I am having to take some pretty tough decisions on people like that on where and how I can use them in the future.'

(b) *What is the best practice for a Management Accountant working with this type of system?*

The Management Accountants need to understand the data, analyse it and gain insights from it, and then communicate that information to Senior Managers in such a way that they are first alerted and, second, can act on that data when they are ready. **The Management Accountants need to become business partners, and leave report generating to the software.** They must also make sure the ERP does not shower the business with irrelevant data just because it can. It is about being smart (as always).

(c) *What guidance would you provide for Management Accountants in organisations that have recently implemented ERP systems?*
- It is very hard work, especially if it has been on top of an increased business as usual agenda. Need to re-energise frequently and be aware that some may fall by the wayside.
- Must develop a business partner perspective, not just a reporting view.
- Be prepared for a shift towards more forward-looking analysis, where synthesis and analysis skills are essential, must get the big picture.
- Communication needs to be effective and in a format that senior management can understand. It has to withstand the 'so what' challenge and be engaging and decision relevant.
- Need to understand the data architecture, and take steps to make sure your managers and analysts can get out the data they need. It would be tragic to have gone to the trouble to create such a powerful database and not fully leverage it.

Summary

Management Accountants do need to be involved in ERP implementations. DDD did not involve key Management Accountants (those able to understand the Group, Region, Company, and business process perspectives) at the right level at the start of the project. Subsequently, during the 'rebuilding' stage, Management Accountants who were able to provide analysis and decision support skills were involved. This has resulted in DDD being able to scale the data from a country level to a company level and create a data warehouse that provides significant data analysis capabilities. Further, **there was a 40% reduction in staff** (from 55 to 33) since the more clerical tasks performed (e.g. statutory accounting) have been automated. DDD has also implemented a service centre for accounting activities and is closing individual country/location accounting offices.

Organisations that are going to introduce an ERP system must be prepared to re-engineer their business processes (especially their data definitions and accounting, reporting and analysis models). Also, there must be discipline in the system use. This means that all the operational level system users must participate and must use the new system in the proscribed manner once it is implemented.

It has taken over 2 years, but the ERP software is finally providing significant benefits for DDD, especially in the finance area. This turnaround occurred through '*stealth re-engineering*' and focusing on getting a series of small wins and fixes which, in the aggregate, resulted in a significant payback; and through the leadership of the group financial controller who insisted that everything that was done needed a business focus.

Case E

This company (EEE) is a global food and consumer products company with sales in over 100 different countries and is listed on stock exchanges worldwide. Three senior managers from the accounting and R&D areas participated in the interview, a Finance Manager, a Research & Development Manager (R&D Manager) and a Management Accountant.

Background

The three interviewees were interviewed separately at a Research and Development (R&D) site of EEE. This R&D site is different from a 'traditional' production or operational customer site –no inventory, no manufacturing and no sales – and the majority of the employees have PhDs in their areas of specialisation. This leads to unique problems, as these individuals are generally very independent and confident in their skills in any area (even if they have no experience in that area, such as ERP systems). In addition, the focus of this site is on developing and improving consumer products rather than producing or selling those products. The accounting system is primarily used to develop budgets, provide information about proposed projects and the control of the expenditures for current projects. Further, a significant investment in fixed assets exists at this location.

EEE implemented SAP in 1999, 2 years before the current Finance Manager was appointed. Prior to SAP, Oracle Financials were used. The decision to move to SAP was based upon a desire to standardise on one platform throughout the company worldwide. At this location, EEE implemented the following SAP Version 4.0D modules – FI (including a large Fixed Assets segment), CO and MM (implemented only for the procurement of non-production inventory). Consultants were involved in the initial implementation. They performed 'path clearing' activities leading to the implementation, the close of the old financial system and the 'go live' activities. The consultants withdrew after the system was live.

At the R&D location there are only about 50 'direct' SAP users. The majority of the other users access the SAP system via a web-based application suite (for orders, expense claims and account management). The web interface was developed to improve ease of use and reduce the number of licenses required. Since the initial implementation, SAP has been transformed into a single shared system for all the Research sites, a Global Infrastructure group, an Information Technology Shared

Services Centre and it is used throughout Europe and North America. The R&D Manager mentioned that the current SAP environment at this site is viewed as lagging being those at other locations. There are plans to upgrade this version in the near future so that it is consistent with those used at other locations.

At this location, EEE concentrated on the 'back office' activities, such as procurements, fixed asset accounting, financial accounting requirements and management accounting reporting. SAP was implemented in a *relatively* 'plain vanilla' manner, using a Cost Centre hierarchy within the CO module that matched the current operations. However, the Finance Manager believed that not enough re-engineering occurred and that too many 'work arounds' were implemented in the original SAP installation. The initial implementation team '*basically worked around solutions instead of taking a full vanilla. For instance, they should have had a fully legislated Procure to Pay Process, work that out thoroughly and arranging the other processes. Our Assets Module is incredibly complicated. It should work, from my point of view, on an Assets and a Construction basis whereby everything goes through real internal orders. It didn't until very recently and we still have a convoluted system...*'

The R&D Manager concurred with this assessment. He stated that the Management Accountants set out what they wanted to do and did not have anyone challenge them. Effectively, they had too strong an influence on the design of the implementation and, as a result, the existing processes were implemented without any significant re-engineering. The effects of this could be seen in the average age of payables, which was 89 days when the Finance Manager started. It is now less than 40 days as a consequence of workflow and process improvements having been initiated. The R&D Manager viewed the match between SAP and the business orientation as a '2' on a scale of 1 (no match between the ERP software orientation and the business orientation) and 7 (complete match). The Management Accountant concurred, and also viewed it as a '2' on the 7-point scale.

End user decision support is accomplished through a web-based reporting tool that provides both 'snap shot' and 'drill-down' capabilities into the appropriate SAP module. The casual users (researchers) are not interested in understanding an ERP system; they need a quick and efficient method to determine their remaining budget, how much money was spent, and what the money was spent on. The web-based tool provides an easy to use graphical user interface and obviates the need to purchase additional SAP seat licenses for these casual users. A more traditional 'monthly accounting' is performed at the R&D location rather than 'real-time accounting' since a significant portion of all costs are labour-related and these occur on a monthly payroll cycle, as is the fixed asset accounting. Procurement costs are relatively minor and are dealt with as they occur.

The R&D Manager considered the implementation a success, but that was based on the observation that they had to install SAP and that it was functional. His comment was tempered by the comment that **he had not seen any type of post-analysis or financial analysis on the impact of the system.**

The Finance Manager believed that the original ERP system was implemented in a poor fashion. He stated that a successful implementation would have concentrated on re-engineering the business processes and *'and making sure that everyone had a good understanding of the processes and the part they play in the processes.'* The design needed more expert involvement and should not have involved any changes to the software. Early problems with Invoice Processing were used as an exemplar: *'I couldn't guarantee that I was right and I had a £1 million in some 900 transactions every month not allocated to my ledgers. Quite appalling! And that is through bad process engineering, that they hadn't looked at their business processes properly and made sure that all parts were aligned and that they actually did hold together well.'*

Although the initial implementation was viewed as lacking, the Finance Manager stated that the current (revised) system is a mixed success from the management accounting perspective. It is used to control financial affairs, it provides relevant and reliable information and enough analytical data for decision support purposes. The primary weakness is that it is not much of a budgeting tool. Despite the Sarbanes–Oxley and other corporate governance implications, spreadsheets are still extensively used, and are still used as a reporting tool. However, they are currently going through Sarbanes–Oxley implementation and *'we have the benefit by using SAP as our ERP in that all of the work that has been done to look at process compliance and control checks, etc, in the major SAP environment… and we can piggy back [this] work that [has been] done elsewhere.'*

The Management Accountant viewed the original SAP implementation as a partial success *'because I don't think that in certain areas of what we do were thought through before it was implemented and we are now stuck with ways of doing things that are overly complex, outmoded and very difficult to unravel and rectify.'* This is consistent with the observation of the Finance Manager and R&D Manager that much more re-engineering of the management accounting process was needed.

Another concern of the Management Accountant was *'the knowledge drain that people leaving and restructuring it [the ERP system] is becoming less of a success by the day as we find that…there are things that we want to do that we can't do because we either haven't got the knowledge or we haven't got an up-to-date enough system to do it.'*

The Finance Manager stated that data for spreadsheets is generally obtained electronically from SAP via *'snapshots'*, or by importing data that are then manipulated. Data is also uploaded into SAP through web-based interfaces for purchase requisitions and expenses. About 20% of the work of the 10 individuals performing transaction processing is done outside of SAP. However, **about 80% of the work of the five Management Accountants is performed outside SAP.**

The R&D Manager concurred with the view that the Management Accountants were not using the full capabilities of SAP and that the majority of the work is performed using data pulled from the system and dumped into Excel.

The Management Accountant agreed with these assessments. He stated that SAP was mainly used as a '*drill down*' tool. For management purposes, Excel is used a lot and '*we are downloading stuff and jigging it around. Whereas, what we would really like to be doing in the future is using the generic reports or reports written especially for us within SAP so we are not having to upload, download and messing about on stuff.*'

The ERP system (after modifications to the initial implementation) has enabled significant improvements in both performance and compliance. The Finance Manager observed that '*we have engineered compliance by not using a big stick, we have made it very easy for the end-user customer to be compliant. For instance, we used to have paper-based expenses system, we knew where the paper was in the system, we knew what had happened to problems, it took us an age to actually process them because the end-user was entering data onto the form. We would then [be] taking that data and entering it onto the accounting system and then we were making the process. Whereas we moved to an electronic system whereby the data was only entered once from that source and my Accounts Payable staff instead of doing data processing, they moved to Systems Administration. As a result of that, I reduced my head count by half; this was twice as effective as it had been in the past. The customers liked it because they had visibility and I got my downstream compliance and also more accurate information and stopping being criticised for losing things. So it was good accountability, good visibility and massive improvement in process efficiency. That couldn't have been enabled within the old ... system; it simply wasn't technically able to cope with that. Whereas one of the good things about SAP is it is quite straightforward to get information in and out of it and particularly where we have electronic interfaces and e-commerce solutions, it is providing a very flexible framework for that.*'

The Finance Manager stated that the R&D site is '*...currently at the lead end of the ARIBA e-commerce solution.*' Significant resources were expended in '*...building interfaces and business processes to connect the ERP system with ARIBA but not to detract from SAP functionality.*' And a hard line was drawn in terms of what was included, as '*... the Procurement people wanted to have the ARIBA system dealing with everything and it just posting the end result transaction into SAP and rather than integrating it with SAP.*' Furthermore, Procurement only wanted changeover to be a feature of ARIBA and not SAP, which would have led to inconsistent data between the systems. The Finance Manager insisted that the data remain consistent, and an interface which complemented the SAP functionality.

EEE (from an overall company perspective) wants to reduce supply chain cost by £1.3 billion. As the Finance Manager explained, '*One of the things that ARIBA and, as a consequence, SAP does for us: ARIBA can sit on top of our various ERP systems and take the same data so we now have a global view of what we are spending by Merchant category for instance. Massively powerful! Without ERP flexibility, we wouldn't have been able to do that.'*

In summary, all three participants viewed the initial system implementation as less than completely successful for the following reasons:

(a) It did not go far enough in business process re-engineering.

(b) Too many 'work-arounds' were permitted.

(c) The team did not have a good understanding of the processes and their role.

(d) Inadequate knowledge management and subsequent 'loss of expertise' when knowledgeable employees left.

(e) It needed more expert involvement.

(f) Consultants were not skilled enough.

(g) Improved training was needed.

(h) SAP was not viewed as a strategic information system when initially implemented.

All three participants also agreed that the ERP system has improved and has provided some benefits for EEE. The SAP system is also viewed as providing an infrastructure, which will provide significant benefits in the future.

The role of the Management Accountants

The previous Finance Director championed the SAP implementation at this location. The implementation team was led by a Management Accountant, and included consultants and technical staff. The team examined business processes, performed limited re-engineering and ensured that SAP was properly configured for the processes. However, the functional design needed more expert involvement and, as implied by the R&D Manager, less influence from the Management Accountants. The Finance Manager made the observation that the '*consultants were learning at the same time as we were and as a consequence we were not well advised*' and that the team '*basically worked around solutions.*'

Use of the system by the Management Accountants

There are five Management Accountants at this site. They perform a mixture of financial and managerial accounting activities. This ensures that the data is integrated between finance and management; there are no financial accountants at the site. The Management Accountants use SAP and have experienced a change in their tasks since the implementation of the ERP system.

However, about 80% of the work performed by the Management Accountants is outside the ERP package. The Finance Manager stated that '... *when they are doing local decision support, what ifs, etc., budgeting that is all done through Excel and we also for things like Payroll and Human Resource information use Access.*' The Management Accountant agreed with the Finance Manager and stated that '*when I was in charge of Accounts Payable as well... Pretty much everything to do with Accounts Payable came out of SAP, so that would be Productivity Reports right through to Query Resolution all came through SAP. On the Management Accounts side probably about 80% would be in Excel, so that would be budgeting, funding and so on, incoming information. Management accounts information going back out again is only about 20% and that would just be looking at the variance reports in SAP.*'

The R&D Manager didn't think that the Management Accountants really embraced the ERP system. In his opinion, '*...they treat it as a data engine that has got some mechanical abilities*' and that they really don't understand all of the capabilities of the ERP system. The Management Accountants are using SAP as a large database and a limited reporting tool. The R&D Manager lamented the lack of support for employees using SAP. There is only one 'super-user' on site, and that individual isn't a SAP consultant, nor does that individual attend training courses, conferences or any other method to pick up tips and hints on how to best utilise SAP. The R&D Manager hoped that the recent establishment of a '*Help Desk*' would improve the situation.

The changing role of the Management Accountants

Prior to the implementation of the ERP system, the R&D unit had financial accountants and managerial accountants who were all part of a finance function that was over staffed, inefficient, ineffective and not good value for the money. The ERP system helped transition to an environment in which more time is spent on decision support and business partnering and less on transaction processing and financial accounting.

The Finance Manager stated that **the role of the Management Accountants had changed dramatically after the implementation of the ERP system**. '*...when I joined, the Management Accountants were Budget Buddies if you like. They would get together with their customers and work through budgets, they would produce the odd report for them and that would be the end of it. They are much more now focused on Business Partnering and what I would say the ERP system has done is liberated a lot of them from the transactional and the technical and given them more time to spend on decision support which is the kind of human interface work... [and] the* *quality of the input and the professionalism has changed markedly.*' The Finance Manager also commented that each of the five Management Accountants help manage, '*…£20 million roughly each, that is a small to medium sized enterprise in it's own right and my guys act, my Management Accountants act as Finance Directors for their area. They look at strategy, business planning, budgeting, decision support, what if scenarios, risk, avoidance, risk, all of the things that a small company FD would be into.*'

The R&D Manager had a very different perspective. He stated that **there was significant turnover in the Management Accountants** (he thought that only one Management Accountant remained who participated in the original rollout of SAP). However, his view was '*…that the way they do it hasn't substantially changed. So I will get a spreadsheet showing the top level for the cost centres I am responsible for and the breakdown at a very high level with a lot more detail in it.*'

With respect to things that could be done now that couldn't have been done in the past, the Management Accountant observed that the volume of transactions that can be examined just by running a report compared to the old more manual system had risen. Additionally, since the SAP system has strong internal controls, the potential to overrule things that should not be overruled is virtually eliminated versus having more of an opportunity to do that on a more manual system. The MA also stated that with hindsight, '*I would learn more about SAP and the reports it has and then try and get to the answers I want through SAP rather than manipulating the data outside of SAP after the event.*' He would prefer to utilise the capabilities of SAP rather than downloading the data into Excel to perform some of the required analyses.

The extent to which the new system has had an impact on the role of Management Accountants on the following functions was described as follows:

The scores relate to the question: 'On a scale from 1 to 7 (1: very much reduced to 7: very much increased).'

(a) *Time spent on data collection* **Score = 1**

The Management Accountants spend significantly less time on 'data collection.' In the past, they would need to go through over 900 invoices at month-end, review, determine if they were material (they did not have a purchase order number quoted on them) and approve them. They also had to identify who raised the order and the appropriate cost centre. This resulted in many manual accruals. They now make very few manual accruals.

(b) *Time spent on data analysis* **Score = 2**

The Management Accountants do not need to analyse the data to verify that it is recorded correctly. According to the Finance Manager, 'So if you have good process compliance through that business process, the Management Accountants have to do a lot less work, a lot less re-work and they do a lot less re-work.' The MA observed 'Yes, I think it [SAP] has taken a lot of messing about with the presentation out of it. It has automated a lot of that so that we can concentrate more on just decision support. Theoretically, even with the limited functionality we have, we should be able to dump a report that tells us everything that we need to do in a few mouse clicks so it has taken the slog out of that. Management Accounting...in the future, that could go even more so. There is a lot more automation speeding up we could do so Management Accountants can spend less time looking at errors basically within the system and more time concentrating on strategy in meetings, etc.'

(c) *Involvement in business decision-making* **Score = 7**

Involvement in business decision-making and business partnering has gone up 'massively'

(d) *Focus on internal reporting, for example performance measurement and control issues* **Score = 6**

Control has gone up.

(e) *Focus on external environment (e.g. benchmarking)* **Score = 2**

The MA interpreted this question to mean 'standard' financial-type reporting and stated that external reporting is standardised, that the time spent has gone down. The Finance Manager's perspective was on benchmarking the R&D centre performance relative to other internal sites, to be able to evaluate their relative efficiency and effectiveness. Beyond that, the organisation has become more local rather than regional as it was before due primarily to divisional reorganisation within EEE.

The following summarises the response to the questions listed below:

(a) *To what extent are traditional analysis performed that focus on past operating results compared to decision support type of analysis that have a forward-looking focus?*

There is an increase in forward-looking analyses. The Finance Manager stated that '*The now and future element is probably again a good 80%. Not a lot of time looking backwards.*' Prior to the ERP implementation there was about a 50% backward-looking focus. The MA stated that his job was now '*60/40 in favour forward looking.*' In the past, the job would have been much more backward looking, about 70% backward looking.

(b) *Are the Management Accountants performing cross-functional analysis compared to domain specific analysis?*

The Management Accountants are doing more cross-project work than individual projects. The Finance Manager stated '*We operate a complete matrix structure here that on the one hand we have income flowing or funds flowing into us from the 5 categories we support. But then that is actually distributed through something like 16 groups from different scientific specialisations... [The management accountants] spend an awful lot of time in terms of working through that matrix structure and forward planning stuff in terms of putting people on projects and costing that through, working out average full-time equivalence and they spent a lot of time on that. A lot of time looking towards the plan for the coming year and in budgeting.*'

The Management Accountant didn't see a significant change. However, his perspective concerned whether one participated in cross-functional or domain specific analysis depended upon the task, or group that he was working with. If Management Accountants were working with Group Managers, the focus would be within the domain since that is what the Group Managers focus on. However, if they were working with the Leadership Team or the Finance Director, they would take a cross-functional perspective.

(c) *Since less time is needed for data capture and less time is spent generating routine reports for managers, what are the Management Accountants doing with the extra time?*

According to the Management Accountant, they are becoming more involved in '*...in decisions about resourcing and external spend and annual plans...*' He also stated that more time is spent on strategic planning, writing proposals and analysis for one-to-three years ahead that was not done in the past.

(d) *Have the communications skills of the Management Accountants become more significant and important than they were before?*

The communication skills are important. The Management Accountant needs to be able to interpret and provide the information to the users in a manner that the managers understand. **The focus is now much more on what the data means and where the group can go in the future**, whereas in the past the communication was primarily reviewing what happened.

(e) *Has the formal or informal communication structure involving the Management Accountants changed as a result of the new system implementation?*

Prior to the implementation of SAP, the communication structure was much more formal and followed a tighter routine. This was necessitated by the length of time required to obtain and distribute the information. Prior to the implementation of the ERP system, ad hoc analysis was virtually impossible. The Management Accountant now generally provides hard copy reports to the management team when they meet. This facilitates discussion rather than only having soft-copy reports. The Management Accountant provides an interpretation of the graphs/reports to the management teams.

(f) *How satisfied were the Management Accountants, both prior to and post the new system implementation?*

Prior to the SAP system, the Management Accountant stated that he would probably have been about 50% satisfied with his job, whereas now he was closer to 75% satisfied. He had been an auditor prior to joining EEE and had not been involved in the SAP implementation, so his response is based upon his understanding of the organisation prior to his employment. He also stated that he preferred the work at EEE to working in auditing, as he felt a lot more involved in the business on an on-going basis.

(g) *How have the Management Accountants contributed to the success of the new system?*

The Management Accountants and the Finance Manager were critical for the success of the system. In addition, those involved in the implementation of the ERP system are also critical to the day-to-day success of the system. The Management Accountant stated, '*in the past the Management Accountants have managed the knowledge of actually how to actually do it. I know the two ex-Management Accountants who were still here when I joined, have since left, were involved with the implementation so they had been right there from the start and when they left most of the SAP knowledge went out with them.*'

The changing role of the Management Accountant in successful/unsuccessful Implementations

The Finance Manager observed that in a successful ERP implementation '*Management Accountants can focus much more on managerial issues, more commercial and more decision support. Whereas the Financial Accountant becomes specific and more expert in that particular area of responsibility. …It allowed the Management Accountants to get on and do their job, if you like service level agreements in place to make sure that the Financial Accountants were doing their job and that they had relevant, reliable information and data which to make informed decisions. With a less successful implementation, the …distinction would be blurred and you would find duplication of effort on it and also lack of responsibility.*'

The R&D Manager believed that there would be a significant difference, that in '*a very successful implementation there would be less routine work, there would be less of the financial accountancy work that they currently do but are responsible for and there would be more of the customer interaction work... [and] they would be a partner rather than just a supplier.'*

At present, within EEE, the Management Accountants have a higher perception of themselves in terms of their effectiveness and support that they provide compared to how their customers view them.

The R&D Manager stated that Management Accountants should educate Middle Management how to better use the ERP system. The Middle Managers need to be able to control budgets and spending, and process knowledge of the ERP system would enable them to do, especially process analysis, would be helpful. He also stressed the importance of *'Customer Service'* for the Management Accountant. They need to know their customer and spend some time with them, not just show up for a 1-hour meeting once a week. The Management Accountant needs to acquire the *'institutional knowledge'* of their clients, and that is only obtained by spending time doing work at the client site.

Recommendations for Management Accountants

The following summarises the responses to the questions (listed below) about recommendations for Management Accountants involved in the implementation and use of ERP systems.

(a) *What skills would you recommend for Management Accountants that have recently implemented ERP systems?*
- Be qualified, either CIMA or ACA (professional credence is needed in this location because of the large number of PhD and other qualified customers with whom the Management Accountant must interact; source credibility is important).
- Good technical basis.
- Must understand business processes: *'ERP systems are bloody complicated. If something goes wrong, establishing cause and effect is difficult.'* (Finance Manager)
- Good interpersonal skills.
- Good analytical skills, need to know what you are looking for and need the ability to find out on your own to know what questions to ask to get somebody else to find it.
- Manage and hold others accountable for decisions.
- Educate the customer to the way Management Accountants provide value.
- Be involved from the concept of a project, rather than at the end.

- Adaptive intelligence, depending on their role in the team, technical skills and good software skills (with the ability to adapt).
- Leadership skills.
- Change management skills.
- Be able to spot things that are wrong and have an idea of how to fix them.
- Ability to learn quickly.

(b) *What is the best practice for a Management Accountant working with this type of system?*

The Management Accountant needs patience, persistence and discipline within the ERP environment. In addition, they need to be aware of controls like segregation of duties, and in a team setting to make sure that they are doing things in a legitimate manner. Further, according to the Management Accountant, Management Accountants need to *'find out what they need to do on a routine basis and make sure that they are able to do that as quickly and as trouble free as possible. To keep an open mind for as long as possible about improvements that they could make.'*

(c) *What guidance would you provide for Management Accountants in organisations that have recently implemented ERP systems?*

There are weaknesses in any system, and rather than becoming accustomed to them, they should always be pushing to eliminate the weaknesses, for continuous improvement. They should avoid getting stuck with a backlog of half-finished things in the system – this can be particularly troublesome if the system is onerous to use and not many people understand it.

Summary

This case focused on a very different environment for the Management Accountants: an R&D site for a global company. The Management Accountants were involved in the initial implementation of SAP at this location. The senior people interviewed both believed that the initial implementation simply implemented the then current business practices, and did not include re-engineering that would have resulted in significant improvements. The R&D site is now in the process of implementing gradual improvements and re-engineering the processes one at a time. So, while the implementation is a success, it is not as successful as it could have been.

The role of the Management Accountant has changed, but not as dramatically as it could have changed if there was a more successful ERP implementation. There has been significant turnover in the staff and much SAP knowledge has left the organisation. There is extensive use of Excel for data analysis. The Management Accountants' task is now more forward-looking, and whether it is cross-functional depends upon the task at hand. The R&D Manager did not perceive as much of a change in the Management Accountants' tasks as did the accounting professionals. He did, however, note that there was a positive change in the self-perception of the Management Accountants – that they perceived themselves more as business partners providing significant value for managers.

Case F

This company (referred to as FFF Limited) is a large-listed company in the automotive industry. The case study perspectives on the implementation and use of the ERP system were provided by the Chief Financial Accountant, the Chief Management Accountant, the Purchasing Engineer, and the IT Systems Administrator.

Background

FFF is a leading provider of technology and engineering services to the automotive industry worldwide. It is a large UK-listed company which employs over 1700 people in technical centres throughout the world. The company's customer base includes the leading automobile manufacturers (OEMs) worldwide. FFF has had a fourfold growth since it implemented its ERP system, and the head count in support areas such as finance and systems has grown at a slower rate than the corporate growth.

FFF implemented BAAN in September 1999 mainly motivated by the Year 2000 problem. Several modules of the BAAN system were implemented, including financials, manufacturing and warehouse. A 'big bang' implementation strategy was followed: the entire company went live at the same time and for all modules.

FFF was among the first companies in the UK to implement BAAN. The IT Systems Administrator stated that the initial version of BAAN was very unstable, and that '*I was putting patches on, kind of 20, 30 patches a day with hundreds of pre-requisites, and it was just fire fighting for the first two years, it was really awful.*' FFF subsequently upgraded to the next release of BAAN which was much more stable.

Implementation of the BAAN system took approximately 10 months. In addition to the Year 2000 problem, the implementation was motivated by a lack of trust in the old system and the manufacturing orientation of the organisation that demanded an understanding of product costing. Additionally, the Finance Director wanted a system he could use without having to rely on everyone to provide him with the needed information.

The project team varied from seven to nine internal FFF people: the Chief Management Accountant, and one person each from Finance, Manufacturing, Logistics, Stores, Projects, a part-time person from Warehousing, and a part-time person to support projects and training. The Financial Director was the project champion, manager and in charge of commercial negotiations. Group Finance was represented, and eventually the Group Internal Auditor joined the team. In addition, a similar number of consultants were involved. The consultants were initially from a consulting firm. After 3 months, these consultants were replaced with consultants from BAAN.

The Finance Director had overall responsibility for the implementation, and he was heavily involved in all the project costings and in how the project team operated. The Chief Management Accountant was heavily involved in the implementation. There was also an accountant brought in from another division with previous exposure to implementing systems, in order to 'project manage' the implementation.

The project had complete support from top management. The Financial module is perceived as the most successful module whereas the Manufacturing and Warehousing modules still had unresolved issues.

A limited amount of business process re-engineering was undertaken in response to the BAAN implementation. In other words, since BAAN undertook processes differently, some of the processes were changed to meet the BAAN method. The Chief Management Accountant stated that we '*tweaked our procedures to fit in with the system*' but, apart from that, there wasn't any significant re-engineering of the business processes. He expressed the view that some of the processes that BAAN employs, especially in warehousing, created problems.

The Chief Management Accountant and Chief Financial Accountant were the main accountants involved in the implementation, although the Chief Financial Accountant was not a member of the project team. It was their job to sell the idea that BAAN was going to help them to get information out to managers. There are four additional Management Accountants in FFF who have responsibility for project accounting, the BAAN system, ensuring that all the transaction postings are valid, and for the costing side of the business. They are also responsible for budgeting and forecasting. The Financial Accountants are responsible for the purchase ledger, sales ledger and payroll.

Formal training on the new system was provided by BAAN. The Chief Management Accountant stated that the training sessions at the start were quite good, but became weaker as the specific courses lacked documentation and gaining suitable experts was difficult.

According to the Chief Management Accountant, FFF attempted to '*play with the configurations to make it work the way that we wanted it to.*' This was done with the help of the on-site consultants, who were also going through a learning curve because they had used a previous version of BAAN, not the newer version FFF were using: '*BAAN were educating themselves as they were training us.*'

The project team took ownership of the implementation. There were three stages in BAAN's target methodology:

(1) Decide on the processes to be used with BAAN, present the basics of those processes to FFF and map the process to BAAN.
(2) The project team (supported by the consultants) presented the processes and system use to the FFF users.
(3) The decision they had to be made to go live or not: '*we are using the system very effectively, we are happy with the configuration, and away we go.*'

As far as the user community was concerned, the project team demonstrated the processes to users. The project team gained feedback by asking: 'Are you happy with this?' 'Are the controls in place?' 'Is the output as appropriate?' The Chief Management Accountant stated that, at the time of deciding to go live, '*in principle, I'd say that people were happy.*'

The Chief Management Accountant was the main finance person involved in and responsible for the implementation. The Financial Controller was also involved in the implementation, in particular for setting up codings, ensuring that all the accounts were established correctly and training all the people to use it within the Finance Division.

The Chief Financial Accountant did not consider the implementation to be a success at time of implementation. He stated, '*the software didn't really do what they said it would do.*' Now, he considered it to be more successful. The initial impact of BAAN on the organisation was '*horrendous.*' Now, through the use of external tools to retrieve information from the BAAN system, the Chief Financial Accountant considered that it is looked on with a lot '*more favour.*' He considered it to be the '*system controller across the rest of the group.*'

Initially, many people worked around the system because they could not get it to work properly. Now, they do follow and use the BAAN system. When the BAAN system went live, everyone expected it to work properly '*you know, we spent a fortune on it*', but it didn't, people lost faith and the attitude developed, '*Why should I use it when I can use a spreadsheet instead.*' Now, they are returning to the system and the Finance Director has been pushing hard for it to be used.

The implementation was now seen by the Chief Financial Accountant to have the following impact on the company:

(a) While there has not been a substantial reduction in inventory levels, the BAAN system has provided a better visibility of inventory levels. Since the company manufactures to order, the BAAN system had some limited impact on inventory and inventory turnover.
(b) There has not been a reduction in the number of employees.

(c) A 'good impact' on:
- Order management and cycle times
- Procurement costs
- Cost management
- Productivity (at least 'some' impact)
- Customer service
- Ability to respond to change – The example given was that the company had taken on other divisions who had gone onto the BAAN system 'without any hassle.'
- Improved decision-making and planning

(d) Little impact on cost reduction in overall operations since in manufacturing, there is a problem with understanding how much products are costing.

In contrast to the Chief Financial Accountant, the Chief Management Accountant (who was part of the project team) considered that his perception of the success of the BAAN system was that it was now less successful than when they went live in 1999. These comments need to be placed into the following context. The BAAN system is helping to better manage the company. The key word is 'perceived.' FFF's situation is that they now know more about the strengths and limitations of the software, and as such can identify what they want/need to do yet cannot be easily accomplished within BAAN. Hence, the perceived success has declined even though FFF is operating the software more successfully than when it was originally implemented.

The Chief Management Accountant described FFF's organisation culture as flexible and democratic as compared to bureaucratically controlled.

On a scale of 1–7 (where 1 is not successful and 7 highly successful) the Chief Management Accountant provided the following perceptions:

Module	On implementation	Now
Financials	4	3 or 4
Manufacturing	3 or 4	2
Warehouse	4	3
Tools	4+	4
Projects	4−	4

As mentioned earlier, the Chief Management Accountant considered that, even thought they understand BAAN better and have introduced improvements to the software that enabled FFF to run it more effectively, his perception of the BAAN ERP system had worsened since implementation. So while the company was actually 'happier' with BAAN now than when they went live, the Chief Management Accountant ranked the perception of the success of each module as now being lower.

This appears to have been because of high expectations for the new system that can now be seen to have failed to materialise but which could not be assessed effectively when the system went live. For example, with the Projects module which, '*we thought was a good solid module when we went live [but,] as we've used it we've identified weaknesses in it: specifically, reporting foreign currency transactions and the way that the module handles them; but we didn't know that at the time.*' This obscuring of the reality of the capabilities of the new system arose partly because FFF went live in September 1999 with a system they were still testing, that had hit a '*bug wall because it was new software, [and had] had loads of bugs fixed*' because Year 2000 was only 3 months away, '*which is not [a] perfect [way to do things].*'

BAAN provides thousands of standard reports '*but very, very few of them are usable management tools.*' Other software is used to write reports to extract the data or to use the data warehouse. FFF is using two ways to access the data within BAAN, a 'home-grown' web-based interface and a commercially available 'bolt-on' software package. Despite the Sarbanes–Oxley implications, in some cases users can access the data or reports without having to actually log into BAAN.

In response to the question, 'What, overall, would you say your impression is of the impact of the BAAN system on the organisation', the Chief Management Accountant replied:

> '*OK, from a financial perspective, we have an integrated system: that's good. It enables us to run our business: that's good. There are elements within the organisation that are not happy with the way BAAN works or with the way that it produces its results.*'

The Chief Management Accountant responded as follows to questions about the impact on:

(a) Reduction in inventory levels: 'Some impact.'

(b) Faster inventory turnaround: 'Some impact.'

(c) Change in the number of employees: 'Some impact – down.'

(d) Order management: 'Significant impact – improvement.'

(e) Reduced procurement costs: 'We have had an impact in reducing costs because we are following a standard process that is controlled.'

(f) Improved cost management: No change.

(g) Overall productivity improvement: 'We are a make-to-order business and we employ actual costing as a costing method. Since we've gone live with BAAN, we have a constant shifting bottleneck.' The company now uses a non-BAAN product for schedules. He added, 'The costing system is a mess...'
(h) Customer service improvement: Possibly a little impact.
(i) Delivery time: 'Difficult to quantify.'
(j) Cost in overall operations: 'I've got to say no, because of BAAN the cost of our business system has increased...' and 'BAAN's not a cheap fix. So, in terms of reporting and controlling costs within the business, it probably has led to savings because the information is widely available more easily.'
(k) Better resource management: 'Only in terms of machine utilisation, not in terms of labour.'
(l) Better ability to respond to changes: 'I can see positive and negative influences there. Positive in that we have an integrated system and that we've got access to information; and negative in that because of this particular implementation and the problems we've had with the software, we've had to apply resources to fix those problems, so yes and no.'
(m) Overall improved decision-making and planning: 'One of my objectives is to ensure that the results we produce give our senior management confidence and I haven't passed that one yet.' The Chief Management Accountant considered that the information produced by BAAN is some areas was dramatically improved but not in others.
(n) Overall performance improvements: No.

When asked if, in hindsight whether he would chose BAAN or another ERP system, the Chief Management Accountant stated: '*I don't think it would make a lot of difference.*' On a group-wide basis, they are seriously considering '*dropping BAAN.*' However, he was not convinced that another ERP system would necessarily satisfy FFF, and the next alternative is to develop their own system in-house.

The IT Systems Administrator (interviewee), a computer science graduate, was hired by FFF in July 1999, so only saw the tail-end of the implementation process before the system went live in September 1999. He mentioned that some systems, such as Microsoft Project, were used stand-alone, even though they could be integrated with BAAN.

When asked the question 'how successful do you think the modules are currently rather than on initial implementation, (1 unsuccessful and 7 was very successful), the IT Systems Administrator replied as follows:

'We've had quite a lot of problems with the engineering module so I'd probably say 3 or 4 for that one. Projects have been a fairly successful one, so

that kind or 6 or 7. Finance, we had a lot of problems to begin with, but is pretty stable now, although there's been one or two, with finance rather than there being lots of little problems which we've had in engineering, there's been kind of big, major problems. But the rest of it has run fairly successfully. ... Warehousing has been pretty successful. I'd say kind of 5 or 6.'

On a scale of 1 to 7 (where 1 is not successful and 7 highly successful) the IT Systems Administrator provided the following perceptions of the success of the modules in initial implementation:

Module	On implementation
Financials	4
Manufacturing	3 or 4
Warehouse	5 or 6
Tools	6
Projects	4

Note that this is fairly consistent with view of the Chief Management Accountant, though higher with respect to warehouse and tools.

The IT Systems Administrator confirmed the view that the BAAN system had been released too early and had not been tested properly, which caused problems on implementation. There was a lot of upheaval for the first 2 years, but now it's more stable. The IT staff were assigned the usual tasks: setting up the servers, migrating the data, testing data, checking compatibility; general upkeep of the system, upgrades, attending user meetings to see how and what changes they need to the system.

In relation to the effect on the organisation, his response was:

'People had to ... get out of their old ways of doing things and I think it was quite hard for people to accept that they'd have to change their ways and do some things differently. And also, I think some of the things that were done differently, probably might have took slightly longer, which frustrated them, because [the previous system] was a fairly simple system, and BAAN's obviously quite complex. I think people saw that as just more of a hindrance I think, because some of the processes took so much longer.'

There were also problems in various areas that took a significant amount of time and effort to solve. '... in warehousing we had a problem with stock valuation, stock valuation was out by about eight million or something. So they just couldn't report

Management Accounting in Enterprise Resource Planning Systems

far easier to use. Initially, the engineers, for example, did not *'want to know'*, with the front-end they are using BAAN to retrieve data on their projects. The budgeting tool in BAAN is not used. Budgeting is still done offline on Excel spreadsheets. The data is downloaded into Excel from BAAN. The reason given is that Excel provided a clear format.

The current use of BAAN by the Management Accountants was expressed by the Systems Administrator as follows:

'It's basically a data warehouse. One of the problems we experienced with the project managers was that they were really just using BAAN at the end of the month for the project review forms and they were such infrequent users that they were really, really struggling to kind of remember what do to, and a lot of people complained that the look and feel of BAAN is quite unattractive and difficult to use. So they set up a data warehouse just for the project managers to access all their data, so most of the requests go through for different reports they want and we've had that for a couple of years now and that has made the world of difference. It's kind of a web front end and very easy for them to use - they can get all the data they want.'

The changing role of the Management Accountants

Chief Financial Accountant stated that there had been *'somewhere between some and considerable'* impact of the BAAN system on management accounting and the work of the Management Accountants. He believed it caused a *'different mindset'* and it has led to a better understanding of the business. However, this view was not shared by the other three interviewees.

The Chief Management Accountant considered that the BAAN system has enabled the Management Accountants to *'do more'* than under the previous system. The downside was that, because it is an integrated system, they have more reconciliations to do than previously.

In response to the question, 'Has there been an improvement in the quality of management accounting since BAAN was put in place?' the Chief Management Accountant said: *'Bluntly, yes. It's an integrated system.'*

Although they were *'not happy'* with the costing information, *'at least we can do it and understand it…the depth of information is immeasurable. Compared to old system and the access to it is a hundred times better.'*

He expressed the view that the decision-makers at FFF want the information that is now available from the BAAN system. However, for the first two-and-a-half years after implementation, they received less information than prior to the BAAN system. Now, the system is providing more information, but not the same information as under the old system.

successfully, I think there was lots of fiddling around, with spreadsh[
they couldn't work out just straight from the system as you should b
that case for about three years, it took about three years to solve the

The IT Systems Administrator also stated that the ERP software
basis for e-commerce, that the modules make it easy. E-commerc
been possible with the old software environment. However, FFF ha
mented e-commerce within BAAN at this time. The ERP system a
on accountability, controls and responsibility. The IT Systems Ad[
'*everyone has very specific roles and those roles are defined in B*
lot clearer, a lot more specific.'

The Purchasing Engineer is responsible for all purchasing on
worked at FFF since 1994. He was not part of the implementat[
involved with BAAN from '*a testing point of view.*' He considere
tion to be '*quite torturous*'; and on a scale of 1–7 (where 1 is n[
highly successful), ranked the success at implementation to be
rently 'about 5.'

The Purchasing Engineer responded as follows to questions ab[

Reduction in inventory levels: 'little impact.'

Faster inventory turnaround: 'little impact.'

Change in the number of employees: 'little impact.'

Order management: 'little impact.'

Overall productivity improvement: 'little impact.'

Customer service improvement: possibly a little impact.

The role of the Management Accountants

The Chief Management Accountant was heavily involved in
but the bugs in the software and the inexperience of the consu
ware meant that it was hard to exert an effective influence over
sometimes didn't work as expected. Business processes were
where changes were necessary to fit the requirements of the s[
appears to have been designed initially to enable so far as wa
reports to be produced as under the previous system.

Use of the system by the Management Acc[

A problem retrieving information from BAAN in the format
understand prompted the IT staff to write a front-end. Since

Manufacturing is the key area, and yet they receive very little information. The Management Accountants provide manufacturing with costs by order or project. There is no information on machine utilisation. There are no manufacturing or divisional profit/loss reports. It was expected that these reports would be provided in the next 12 months.

The Chief Management Accountant expressed the view that the BAAN system did not allow the Management Accountants to do their job better.

All budgeting and forecasts were carried out using spreadsheets. BAAN did not have functionality available to input forecasts on projects, but *'its not easy, it's not intuitive, it's not user friendly and the formula that it uses is not the way that we would work.'* Thus, all forecasting is done outside the BAAN system. (BAAN does have a budgetary system which FFF had not yet implemented.)

On the other hand, BAAN has had an impact on performance measurements which has affected the management accounting function. In the previous system, a project manager was given a monthly hard copy printout of all the costs of a project – all mixed up, labour, materials, subcontracts, etc. In the new BAAN system, project managers can access a project on-line and view a summary. They can identify what costs were incurred on a particular activity in a particular period. This, access to information is totally different and this has resulted in a different way of *'running the business.'*

Overall, the Chief Management Accountant was of the view that **the new system had really only affected the extent rather than the nature of the role of the Management Accountants**, in that it created extra control accounts which needed to be monitored. There are more accounting control practices and more interim accounts in operation. The new system had not provided any new performance measurement such as the balanced scorecard. Nor does it provide information for strategic management accounts, in relation to new products or cost simulations. The major impact on management accounting and the role of the Management Accountants was the fact that it was a new system, they have had to learn how to use it and there are more controls and more output. The Chief Management Accountant saw no difference in the type of person he would hire as a new Management Accountant as a result of the new system. **Their role had not really changed.**

The IT Systems Administrator also expressed the view that **the role of the Management Accountants had not changed** since the implementation of BAAN. His response to the questions, 'Has there been an improvement in what management accountants do?' and 'Has the quality of what they produce improved since the ERP system went live?' was a blunt *'no.'*

Despite this view, the IT Systems Administrator considered that a number of the problems had been solved in the last 6–8 months, but there is more testing to be undertaken. The view was also expressed that they were *'getting there slowly'* thanks to the implementation of partner software for report generation, a recommended report tool to go with BAAN. They never use the BAAN report writer because they find it too hard to work with.

When asked 'What would you say has been the overall impact on management control systems as a result of the ERP system?' The IT Systems Administrator responded: '*At the beginning quite a huge impact, but not a positive one.*' '*It's getting a lot better. I think there's still room for improvement there.*'

The IT Systems Administrator expressed the view that there had been a considerable negative impact on the work of Management Accountants, at least to begin with, because there were so many problems it made their jobs quite difficult; and that '*the job hasn't changed much.*'

The Purchasing Engineer did not have a good understanding of the Management Accountants' role, but offered the opinion that the BAAN system had little effect.

Summary

In this company, the implementation was not particularly successful. The ERP software was initially implemented to solve the Year 2000 problem and minimal re-engineering of business processes was undertaken. The software vendor provided a version of the software that was very unstable, so much so that FFF needed to apply 20–30 patches in a day. Further, the software vendor consultants assigned to FFF had minimal experience with the version that FFF was installing. Also, users were not able to get the reports that they needed from the ERP software in a convenient manner. The net effect of all of these factors seems to be a never-ending struggle for the company. In many ways it seems that the new system has produced considerable problems for the Management Accountants. Most significantly, the nature of the role of the Management Accountants has not changed.

Case G

This case concerns one division or part (referred to as GGG) of a very large company in the energy and aerospace industry. A Finance ERP Implementation Manager described the finance module element of the ERP system implementation.

Background

The company has substantial operations in the UK and internationally. Annual revenue is more than £5 billion. The company first started using SAP in 2000. The modules implemented are FI, CO, AM, DS, PS, PP and HR. This case study looks at the implementation of the finance module in one division of the company, GGG.

The implementation described in this case study was undertaken with a full-time project team of four people including the Finance ERP Implementation Manager who was CIMA qualified and had previously worked as a Senior Management Accountant in GGG. The other three were GGG staff with: a project background; a procurement background and the Project Manager, who had an engineering/logistics background. There were no external consultants on the project team. Other staff were included on a part-time basis, including a Sales and Distribution Manager and other accountants. The Project Manager dealt with '*a lot of battles on his own and stayed very focussed.*' There was also an executive who championed the implementation '*who was there just to be wheeled in when it was needed and the thing that the Project Manager struggled with was sometimes getting the business to do what they should do, when they should do it.*'

The business '*...was happy [initially] with the [finance] legacy systems it had*', so finance was implemented after the other modules once it became clear that it was simply too costly and inefficient to continue with the finance legacy systems which were '*nearly falling over*' and by the need to bring the finance function into line with the rest of the division and the company as a whole, which had already moved to SAP. The implementation was done in stages, during 2002 and 2003, with functionality being gradually increased over an 18-month period. Some units within the division migrated to SAP in 2002 with others migrating in 2003.

The division had, therefore, implemented various modules of SAP before the financial module, the SD module being the last to be fully implemented in April 2003, 3 months before the finance module went live within the division in June

2003. It went live at that the behest of management and against the advice of the project team, who felt more time was needed to get it right.

Despite the drive to switch to SAP, a finance legacy system still exists in one unit of GGG but will be switched to SAP within the next 18 months.

SAP was considered to be process-orientated and the company business-orientated (or a combination of business/process). The Finance ERP Implementation Manager considered the match between SAP and the organisational structure to be about 4 (on a scale of 1–7, where 1 is no match and 7 a perfect match): '*We make it match... in our part of the business we are not structured in the most effective way to make the best use of SAP. So we don't work around the system but we have to make the system work for us. So it's not a perfect match.*'

The Finance ERP Implementation Manager (who had been one of the four permanent members of the project team) did not view the implementation as a success: '*I wouldn't have held it up as a completely successful implementation... there is a lot of retrospective work that needs to [be done] to at least re-educate people and we need to develop [a] cross-process training package that gives people that understanding... we will be developing that... and we will have to back-fit it... And what we are doing in the meantime is just... giving them that knowledge when we see that they have done something wrong.*'

There was a lot the Finance ERP Implementation Manager would do differently knowing what she knows now; in particular, making the accountants and finance staff aware of what parts of the processes their activities impact upon in SAP. They also did not do enough thinking about the reporting side of the business and did not standardise the types of reports required for different activities, which led to finance staff '*doing things in lots of different ways... [I'd] get rid of all the cottage industries of all of the Excel spreadsheets and things.*'

'*There was never enough discussion about what the reporting would be. We have ended up producing the same reports, post-SAP that we were producing pre-SAP to the Senior Management. You know they have not been affected. If they hadn't have been aware that SAP had been implemented they wouldn't be able to tell.*'

In achieving this status quo, while the ERP system records the transactions, not many of the reports provided to management are extracted directly from it. The management accounting data is extracted in some form from SAP and, despite corporate governance and Sarbanes–Oxley implications; it is presented in Excel or manipulated outside of SAP. Budgeting and planning is not carried out within the SAP system: '*...all the financial plans are in ... many spreadsheets and they are all lengthily developed, so there is no consistency and standardisation at all.*'

Elaborating, the Finance ERP Implementation Manager indicated that spreadsheets are very much part of the organisation culture: '*they are developed all the time... every time we go through a budget cycle somebody creates a different spreadsheet.*' Ideally, this would have been eliminated by the shift to SAP. However, while none of the ledger accounts are created outside SAP and all of the accounts that are reported therefore balance to SAP, Project Managers (and others) want to see reports in a different format. In order that this may be done, the data is downloaded from SAP to Excel (using SAP's data transfer facility). Established practice within GGG is that these spreadsheets are often customised to make them more acceptable to the person working on them, with obvious risks to the integrity of the information presented.

For corporate reporting, the data is downloaded from SAP to another package via Excel spreadsheets. The SAP implementation does not include the facility to perform segmental reporting and analysis by customer, geographical location and product life, so all this must be done outside SAP after downloading the data held in the SAP system.

The Finance ERP Implementation Manager believed that some Management Accountants *'don't like to use SAP at all.'* For them, SAP stores the central transaction data that they can access and then do most of their work outside of SAP. She considered that 25% of the work of Management Accountants involved use of SAP, with the remainder done outside SAP, on Excel (or other systems).

One of the main reasons why the Management Accountants do not like SAP is loss of control. For example, 'very quickly after the implementation [the management accountants] realised the level of integration this system has and how somebody [who] has nothing to do with that process could really screw up their process for them, which is something that they had never had any experience of before. They were very self-contained before and the only thing that went into the accounts was something they had put in, and suddenly there were all of these other things that could affect the accounts that they were looking at and affect them incorrectly. And they had no power to stop it.'

Successful aspects of the ERP implementation at GGG were described as being:

(a) Things are more visible. For example, understanding the inventory and inventory levels. Management are now more aware of the lead times, and while inventory may not have reduced much, there is now a better ability to supply customers (and to satisfy the customer demands). The new processes that have been implemented with SAP (and all staff have access to the same data) have increased the on-time delivery rate to customers substantially.

(b) The integration is *'much, much better.'* For example, a user can view a transaction in the accounts and easily get back to the source where it was created. This was not so easily done in the legacy system.

The Management Accountant's role

Although the Finance ERP Implementation Manager was involved full-time in the implementation, none of the Management Accountants who would actually be using the system on a daily basis were permanent members of the project team, though some were designated as super-users and trained in the use of SAP and the new business processes. This may go some way to explain why so much work continues to be done outside the ERP system using other software; and why the system is not generally liked by the Management Accountants: they were, effectively, presented with it as a finished product rather than being involved in its design and development.

The changing role of the Management Accountants

The Finance ERP Implementation Manager believes that the role of [all] the Management Accountants will change in time. '*They are getting out [into the business] more... [and] the drive [within the company] is for the accountants to become...a business partner rather than just a bean counter... [However, this change in role] has not happened a lot yet... because I think they are still in that trough at the bottom. I think sometimes... after the implementation you go down rather than improve and I think we have not come out yet fully of that trough so I think there is still quite a lot of time being spent sorting out the things that are wrong. So I see it going up eventually...*'

Expanding on this point, she stated that although the role of the senior Management Accountants has not really changed as a result of the ERP system implementation, it had resulted in some changes for junior Management Accountants who '*no longer have to to register invoices on the system... no longer have to get purchase orders approved... no longer have to actually submit the accounts.*'

The number of Management Accountants was not felt to have changed as a result of the implementation.

The extent to which the new system has had an impact on the role of Management Accountants on the following functions was described by the Finance ERP Implementation Manager.

The scores relate to the question: 'On a scale from 1 to 7 (1: very much reduced to 7: very much increased).'

(a) *Time spent on data collection* 'A little less'	***Score = 2***
(b) *Time spent on data analysis* 'Probably about the same'	***Score = 4***
(c) *Involvement in business decision-making* 'It is starting to go up. A little at the moment'	***Score = 5***

(d) Focus on internal reporting, for example performance measurement and control issues

Score = 2

'It has gone down…medium'

(e) *Focus on external environment (e.g. benchmarking)*

Score = 7

'It has gone up because if they haven't done any of it before and now we are starting.' 'A lot.'

The following summarises the response by the Finance ERP Implementation Manager to the questions listed below:

(a) *To what extent are traditional analysis performed that focus on past operating results compared to decision support type of analysis that have a forward-looking focus?*

'About 70% of their time [is spent] looking back to understand why they haven't achieved what they said they were going to achieve.'
This has not changed since the SAP implementation.

(b) *Are the Management Accountants performing cross-functional analysis compared to domain specific analysis?*

The cross-functional analysis is carried out with systems other than SAP. **There was no change to this.**

(c) *Since less time is needed for data capture and less time is spent generating routine reports for managers, what are the Management Accountants doing with the extra time?*

'They are probably spending more time sorting out the problems than they used to because they didn't have these problems before, you know all the projects that have been set up incorrectly so they are going into the wrong area of their accounts or they are being traded in an incorrect manner or something…'

The Finance ERP Implementation Manager believed that **it was how they were using SAP that had caused the problem**. 'So it goes back to this: making people aware of the integration and how what they do affect somebody else.'

(d) *Has the formal or informal communication structure involving the Management Accountants changed as a result of the new system implementation?*

There tends to be both a formal and informal communication structure within GGG. This has not changed since the implementation of SAP – it is more company culture than the SAP system.

(e) *How happy do you think the Management Accountants, people in that role, are with their job now as opposed to before SAP was put in place?*

'It is difficult to average that out because I can look at two parts of the business and say that it is quite different. The businesses that have been using SAP since the beginning of 2002 I think are happy, they have got a handle on things and they know what is happening. I think parts of the businesses that went [live] in June 2003 haven't come up...they are not happy yet. They are less happy with their role than they were beforehand because they have lost their control and they haven't regained it.'

The extent of satisfaction with SAP was seen partly as a matter of timing. Those that have had more time using the system are more satisfied than those who have not. The view was expressed further as follows: *'It is not SAP that is wrong; it is the people who are putting something into SAP and then doing it wrong; it is not the system, it is the people.'*

The Finance ERP Implementation Manager believes this was not the fault of the Management Accountants, but other users who often lacked training.

In addition to the issue of timing and experience, the units which implemented SAP in 2002 were quite different to those who implemented it in 2003. The 2003 implementation was in selling and distribution units whereas the 2002 implementation was in manufacturing units. The complications and lack of satisfaction arises with the units who sell goods and have to deal with customers. They have not previously had an integrated system with this level of complexity. The example was given of a Manager who was told to delay sending an invoice to a customer but did not realise that the invoice was automatically generated by SAP and would be automatically sent to the customer, causing considerable embarrassment when the customer received it.

The changing role of the Management Accountant in successful/unsuccessful implementations

The Finance ERP Implementation Manager believes that the role of the Management Accountant is very different in a successful implementation as compared to in an unsuccessful implementation. She felt that the implementation was not successful and contrasted what might have been had it been successful with what now exists:

'If you have a successful implementation where you can rely on the information that is in there, you are going to spend far less time having to analyse it and justify it...Whereas, at the moment, we are in a position where we are still questioning here. You get the accounts out and you don't actually have the confidence that you can hand them to somebody else and say, "That is it" without actually doing some detailed analysis to make sure that there isn't any problems with them.'

When asked what the role of Management Accountants would be in a very successful implementation, she responded:

'I think they would be much more focused on strategy type things and helping look at where the business is going rather than what has happened last month. They would look forward more. Perhaps actually getting involved more in the commercial side of the business and the marketing side of the business, a much broader role.'

The Finance ERP Implementation Manager also made the point that anyone who knew how to use the system would be able to make use of its advantages. It may have been a less than unsuccessful implementation, but the problems with it are user-related rather than inherent faults in the system. Management Accountants who were properly trained in its use and who understood the business processes could use the system to their advantage and use it to switch their focus towards the future and towards that of becoming a business partner, as the management of GGG intended. The problem in GGG was that very few users were properly trained in either use of the system or in the new business processes required by the ERP implementation, which is why the overall impact of the implementation of the ERP system on the role of the Management Accountants was minimal.

Recommendations for Management Accountants

The following summarises the response to the following question concerning recommendations for Management Accountants involved in the implementation and use of ERP systems.

What skills would you recommend for Management Accountants that have recently implemented ERP systems?

- IT skills
- Analytical skills
- Communication skills
- Time management skills
- More aware of business processes
- More project focused
- Project management skills
- Integrity

Summary

The implementation of the Finance Module of SAP at GGG was largely unsuccessful. According to the Finance ERP Implementation Manager, much that could and should be being done with the ERP software was being done outside the system with other software, just as had been the case previously; a lot of errors were being made in using the ERP system; but, most of all, there had been a failure in preparing people for the new system and in retraining them in preparation for the roll-out, teaching them both how to use SAP and about the new business processes.

She expressed the view that in a very successful implementation, the role of the Management Accountant would become more strategic, business-oriented, forward-looking and advisory. However, this has not occurred, particularly in those divisions where the SAP implementation occurred later and involved more complicated processes, thus emphasising the lack of success of the implementation.

The suggested skill set needed for a Management Accountant in an ERP environment included more IT skills, a greater understanding of business processes and project management skills. Although analytical skills were seen as important, they were also considered to be essential in a non-ERP environment. As with FFF, in many ways it seems that the new system in GGG produced considerable problems for the Management Accountants, additional time provided by the new system was largely devoted to solving problems created by the system and by the lack of adequate training of users. Most significantly, the nature of the role of the Management Accountants has not changed in a significant way as a result of the ERP implementation.

Lessons learnt

For a variety of reasons, the seven organisations gradually shifted towards using an enterprise resource planning system. Prior to adopting the new systems, operations in all these companies had been traditionally supported through a wide range of non-integrated legacy systems. Generally, with increased competitiveness and growth of businesses, the management in these companies felt the need for a system that would provide cross-functional integration across all business processes through seamless sharing of data across key organisational applications.

In AAA, BBB and FFF, Year 2000 issues were the main driver for the new system; whereas the desire to move to a common standard worldwide was a significant motivator for DDD, BBB, CCC, EEE and GGG. The difference between the organisations in motivations and requirements behind the need of the new system makes it difficult to compare outcomes across them. In particular, in BBB, the major motivator was both the unification of the disparate accounting systems and processes of the business units, and avoidance of Year 2000 problems. As such, the system implementation at BBB was a 'replacement' rather than a 'benefits-driven' case.

The completeness of the ERP implementation and the relative success of the ERP implementation varies across the companies, as does the length of time to implement the ERP system. A strong association was found between the perceived success of the ERP system and the involvement of Management Accountants in the ERP implementation.

However, improvements with regards to the respective metrics used as a measure of success relating to the problems faced by the organisations during and after implementation are important pointers towards the degree of alignment achieved between needs, expectations and results. An organisation-wide ERP system is expected to eliminate the multiple sub-optimal systems typical of legacy systems that generate unstable data, and which are responsible for wasting time of employees, especially the Management Accountants, and top managers. In order to do so effectively, 'ERP implementations must be managed as a program of wide-ranging organisational change initiatives rather than as a software installation effort' (Yusuf et al., 2004, p. 252). In the cases where success was not achieved (in particular, FFF and GGG), the implementations appear to have been treated more as software installation efforts rather than as organisational change initiatives. Also, in the cases that failed, far more of the failure factors suggested by Alioni et al. (2007) and ERP-SELECT (2004) were seen to be present, particularly, inadequate selection of the

ERP project to adopt, low key user involvement, inadequate training and instruction, inadequate business process re-engineering and ineffective consulting services.

The implementation plans in these organisations differed widely, apparently in order to establish a proper alignment with their management structures. In order for an ERP system to succeed, it is important to effectively overcome process- and technology-related issues through clear communication and meticulous execution across the organisation. One of the most important tasks is educating the users of the software, and this is not keystroke training. The users must be educated as to what an ERP really does, and also how their role interacts with everyone else in the system (Wallace and Kremzar, 2001). This is only possible if 'people' issues are tackled properly, by establishing common goals and working together with primary users to change the ingrained culture. In the more successful cases, this appeared to have happened. In those that were less successful, it was less evident. Training in both use of the system and in the new business processes appears to have been a critical factor for success.

Table 4.2 summarises the ERP implementations in the case studies. It also presents the implementation time periods, the overall level of perceived success of the implementation and the corresponding level of change of the role of the Management Accountants. It shows a clear and consistent relationship between the involvement of practising Management Accountants in the ERP implementation and the level of success of each implementation. Similarly, it reveals a clear and consistent relationship between the success of each ERP system and the degree of change in the role of the Management Accountant.

In the very successful ERP implementation of JDE for AAA, the role of the Management Accountants underwent considerable changes. Project management and forecasting jobs have ushered in a higher level of business decision-making into the Management Accountant's portfolios.

BBB wanted to sell-off a major reporting unit consisting of six business units, however disparate accounting systems existed across those business units along with significant Year 2000 problems resulting legacy systems. These business needs were the major drivers for the ERP implementation. After a very slow start, the Management Accountants became major advocates of the implementation. The ERP system fulfils the basic role that was previously performed by the Management Accountants and has empowered them to shift their role from data collectors, data analysers and report producers to Business Accountants with far more involvement in other aspects of the business.

The implementation of SAP at CCC was part of a change strategy aimed at reducing costs. In CCC, the Management Accountants were heavily involved in the implementation, and the implementation is viewed as a success. The ERP system has empowered the Management Accountants to spend more time working with business partners and has enabled them to undertake greater amounts of data

Table 4.2 ERP success –v– Management Accountant involvement in the ERP implementation –v– Change in the role of the Management Accountant

Company	ERP system	Start year	Number of years	MA involvement	Success of ERP*	Change in MA role*
AAA	JDE	1999	1	Yes	3	3
BBB	SAP	1997	2+	Yes	3	3
CCC	SAP	1997	3	Yes	3	3
DDD	SAP	2002	Ongoing	In second phase	2	2
EEE	SAP	1999	Ongoing	In second phase	2	2
FFF	BAAN	1999	0.83	No	1	1
GGG	SAP	2002	1.5	No	1	1

*Scale of success of ERP/change in MA role

3	Significant
2	Moderate
1	Not significant

analysis which, in turn, has led to greatly improved budgetary control and forecasting throughout the organisation.

DDD initially tried to implement SAP around their existing business processes, rather than undertaking any re-engineering. This did not work due to the mismatch between the structures; process-oriented ERP versus function-oriented business. No Management Accountants were involved during this initial phase, and the company ran into problems with regards to usage because of the lack of buy-in from users. Thus the company had to stop its implementation and rethink its strategy. During the second phase initiated by the Finance Department, and with Management Accountants brought on to the project team, DDD was able to gradually simplify some of their business processes and have them match the ERP system. The company has been marginally successful in reaping benefits of ERP, through sharing of data from a common data warehouse and related cost reductions due to automation. In the process, Management Accountants have become more business and strategy focused in their analyses.

The situation at the R&D site of EEE appears to be quite similar to that of DDD. Initial success was plagued due to lack of motivation in re-engineering existing processes, and getting 'stuck with ways of doing things that are overly complex, outmoded and very difficult to unravel and rectify.' Subsequently, gradual improvements were accomplished through re-engineering. However, acquired knowledge also resulted in frustration for the Management Accountants who were not able to do what was required and so failed to realise the full potential of the system. Thus, despite changing to more forward-looking decision-making, the role of the Management Accountants did not change as significantly as it did for AAA, BBB or CCC.

For FFF, the implementation had little positive impact in terms of the changes. Apart from problems arising from minimal re-engineering efforts during implementation, the company also suffered from significant software issues. Not only was the initial software version unstable with new patches released on a daily basis during the initial implementation phase, the consultants provided by the software vendor were learning about the new release at the company site. Thus FFF users never really learned the system, and the new system created more problems than they were able to solve, for the users as well as the management. The role of Management Accountants in FFF has not changed.

In GGG, the success was mixed. In some divisions of the company it worked really well, for others it was less successful. The SAP ERP implementation resulted in more information visibility across the supply chain and an improved level of integration. However, the role of Management Accountants did not change significantly (especially in the units for which ERP did not succeed), since the reports generated through the ERP system still need to be adjusted in a spreadsheet to suit management requirements.

Chapter 5

The Motivations for ERP Deployment

In order to have a competitive advantage (or at least not at a competitive disadvantage), organisations need efficient business processes to better serve the needs of its internal and external customers. When the legacy system is unable to process reliable operations data, and consolidated information becomes inaccessible to management, it has a direct bearing on profitability. An effective software system that will standardise processes, eliminate data redundancy and integrate information across business units is one of the ways to address such problems and one that has been adopted by virtually all the largest organisations in the developed world. Such software systems are known as enterprise resource planning (ERP) systems and have the advantages of reduced cost, rapid implementation and high system quality (Lucas et al., 1988).

Software systems of this type allow easy storage, sharing and retrieval of information and uniform maintenance. For an organisation operating across countries and continents, a global perspective enables it to better serve the world market. In addition, a standardised information system can provide leverage in negotiations with hardware and software vendors. Furthermore, a common IT system across the organisation enables employees to transfer between business units without further training on different IT systems. As shown in Case C, significant savings can be made as a result of a successful ERP implementation – £17.5 million a year, in that case.

However, this type of software requires careful integration across divisions (which could be vastly separated in terms of geography and culture). The design and implementation needs to be managed as a program of wide-ranging organisational change initiatives rather than looked upon as simply a software installation project. As we found, and as supported by previous research, it requires changes 'to the organisation's socio-economic system, which is intertwined with technology, task, people, structure, and culture' (Yusuf et al., 2004, p. 252). 'ERP systems are integrated applications with an impact on the entire organisation' (Aloini et al., 2007, p. 559).

Moreover, the price of consolidating systems must be rationalised against the benefits and ERP systems do not come cheap – £25 million plus would not be unusual for a typical installation in a large organisation. A cost-benefit analysis, along with the specification of system outcomes helps in recognising the successes and failures in terms of post-implementation operational performance measures. But other issues also need to be considered and assessed, not least data and information alignment to business needs and ensuring the buy-in of key work groups – overcoming resistance to change is a critical success factor in ERP implementations (Aloini et al., 2007; Hong and Kim, 2002).

Another critical success factor is the alignment between the data and information needs of the business and the selected software package (Grabski et al., 2001; ERP-SELECT, 2004; Aloini et al., 2007; Grabski and Leech, 2007). Although a package strong in its financials will be a good fit for the financial services industry, a manufacturing- or distribution-focused business needs a package strong in its manufacturing or distribution module, hence the existence of a range of competing ERP products, each of which offers a range of modules from which to build the new system. Organisations need to exercise care in selecting the software package to suit their needs, for mistakes at this stage can be very costly indeed.

As seen from the cases, especially for DDD and EEE (which turned around failing implementations by changing old business processes to match the ERP system processes), the need for re-engineering is obvious and is consistent with prior research (e.g. Grabski et al., 2001). Furthermore, the ERP implementation provides a significant opportunity to address certain critical challenges with regards to alignment of a company's business and IT needs. Trying to fit the software around the existing business process generally results in failure, as does failure of the organisation to switch from a functional focus to a process focus.

Our case studies also demonstrate that the greater the perceived need for the ERP system, the greater the chance of implementation success. When legacy systems are failing, the foreseeable business benefits of a switch to an ERP system are compelling and top management is generally quick to recognise the benefits of doing so. However, changes of this magnitude carry huge implications for everyone involved. Top management needs to not only buy-into the process, it needs to drive it through the organisation, bringing the people with it, sweeping aside inappropriate practices and often completely re-engineering the business and information processes of the organisation in its wake. As shown in our case studies, and consistent with the prior literature (e.g. Grabski et al., 2001; Wallace and Kremzar, 2001) failure to do so is a recipe for failure.

Chapter 6

The Role of Management Accountants in the ERP System Implementation Process

In order for a successful outcome, it is essential that key user groups are involved in ERP projects from an early stage (Wallace and Kremzar, 2001; Aloini et al., 2007; Grabski and Leech, 2007). One of those groups is the guardian of organisation data – the management accountants. Not surprisingly, as ERP systems are dependent upon data, without the involvement and commitment of management accountants to the ERP implementation, the success of the venture is significantly threatened. Senior management that fails to involve them at an early stage does so at the risk of having inappropriate data in inappropriate places and an information system that is even worse than its legacy predecessor.

Our case studies confirm this and demonstrate that management accountants should play a major role in the decision to deploy ERP systems and in the design of those systems. In addition, our case studies suggest that involvement of management accountants in the design stage leads to more appropriate changes being made to the role of the management accountants which, in turn, contributes positively to the success of the implementation. Yet, as we report, key groups such as the management accountants can be overlooked when drawing-up a project team. Although this can be addressed by including them in the project team when making revisions to the system, having to go through a major revision process (as was done in Case D), can be extremely costly for the organisation.

In the three organisations we studied where the management accountants were actively involved throughout the process (AAA, BBB and CCC), a high level of perceived success was achieved (Table 4.2). Significant change also occurred in the tasks performed by the management accountants. The two organisations that delayed involvement of the management accountants until the second phase of the implementation (DDD and EEE) had a moderate level of ERP success, and the management accountants experienced moderate changes in their role. In the case of the two organisations that did not involve the management accountants significantly in the ERP implementation (FFF and GGG), there was limited perceived success of the ERP system and the management accountants continued for some time to perform their tasks as they had prior to the ERP implementation, albeit with different proportions of time being spent on their various tasks.

These findings are supported by previous research which shows that it is critical to get support and buy-in from all users at an early stage through their taking ownership of the ERP system from the start (Grabski et al., 2001). Clearly, user-ownership is easier to cultivate if users take part in specifying how the system should work, and how they will be able to best use the system in their job. Also, since management accountants play a critical role in providing data and information to manage the business, their participation is critical to ensure that the needed data are available and so that the management accountants will know how the data are obtained and reported.

This is most vividly shown by what occurred where the management accountants acted as change agents. That is, where they drove and pushed the changes through the organisation: the system was a success. If the management accountants did not play the role of change agents, the implementation was less successful. In one of the three successful implementations we studied, the interviewee recognised specifically the benefits of their having done so: '*The thing would not have happened if it weren't for them*' (Case B).

In conclusion, management accountant involvement from the start is an essential factor for successful ERP. This message was consistent across all the organisations we studied.

Chapter 7

Advice for Management Accountants in ERP Systems: Implementation, Use and Post-implementation Issues

7.1 Guidance for management accountants

Participants interviewed in all organisations provided insight and advice that they would offer to management accountants of other organisations implementing and using ERP systems. They were asked what they would recommend as 'best practices' for management accountants and they also provided guidance on how management accountants should use ERP systems. The advice offered to management accountants is multifaceted – part of the advice is business-related and part software-related. The advice is summarised in Table 7.1 and discussed later.

Table 7.1 Guidance for management accountants in organisations implementing and using ERP systems

- Have clear objectives.
- Be prepared to listen to others.
- Expect and plan for a productivity dip in the first 2 or 3 months (learning curve).
- Achieve a balance between using external consultants and internal members.
- Don't first rely on external consultants but recognise that those with experience have a contribution to make.
- Obtain support from top management and manage top management's expectations.
- Understand the data architecture and how you can get to the data.
- Make yourself aware of what the software can do. Understand what is possible, what is essential and what is not essential.
- Do as much as possible yourself.
- Challenge traditional reporting.
- Find out what you need to do on a routine basis and make sure that you are able to do these as quickly and as trouble free as possible.
- Change working practices to work with the software (unless there is a good reason for not doing so).
- Use a standardised approach as much as possible.
- Don't get carried away with what the system can do – make it work for you by producing the information you need, not the other way around.
- Do not experiment with things that have not been done by others previously.
- Don't assume the integrity of migrated data.
- Stick with it, keep an open mind, be patient, be persistent, be disciplined.
- Be aware of controls like segregation of duties.
- Keep an open mind about improvements that could be made.
- There will be weaknesses in the system – try to eliminate them.
- Avoid getting stuck with a backlog of half-finished things in the system.
- In using the ERP system, try to empower others, improve data integrity, simplify processes and automate elements of internal control.
- Use the system as a source of information, not as a source of data, that is, as an MIS, not as a data repository.
- Be prepared for a shift towards more forward-looking analysis, synthesis and analysis skills are essential, address the big picture.
- Understand the data, analyse and gain insights from the data.

Table 7.1 Continued

- Communicate your analysis and insights to senior management so that they are alerted and can act on that data.
- Become a business partner, and eschew report generating to the software.
- Attend customer and/or business meetings and demonstrate what a management accountant does and performs.
- For new management accountants, an appropriate introduction to the way the job is done is vital and should include training in use of the system and detailed instruction in the business processes and in how the system interacts with those processes – they need to know how what they do affects and is affected by the system.

7.1.1 ERP Implementation Guidance

From the very start of the implementation, it is important for management accountants to have clear objectives, to be prepared to listen to others and have an open mind. They should expect and plan for a substantial drop in their productivity during the first few months of the implementation. There will be a substantial learning curve and they need to be prepared for this.

There needs to be a balance between using external consultants and internal people during the implementation. The advice was given not to rely entirely on external consultants, but at the same time recognise that those with experience have a contribution to make. It was also deemed important to ensure that top management were supporting the implementation, while at the same time being able to manage the expectations of the top management. This is consistent with success factors from other studies and with the literature.

The importance of being aware of what the software can do and can't do was emphasised. Management accountants need to understand what is possible, what is essential and what is not essential. Within this framework, they should do as much as possible themselves.

Management accountants need patience, persistence and discipline within the ERP environment. In addition, they need to be aware of controls like segregation of duties and, in a team setting, to make sure that they are doing things in a legitimate manner. Further, management accountants need to find out what they need to do on a routine basis and make sure that they are able to do that as quickly and as trouble free as possible. They need to keep an open mind for as long as possible about improvements that they could make. Also, they need to change the traditional way of doing things since it is very likely to be different in the new ERP environment.

There are weaknesses in any system, and rather than becoming accustomed to them, they should always be pushing to eliminate the weaknesses, for continuous improvement. They should avoid getting stuck with a backlog of half-finished things in the system – this can be particularly troublesome if the system is onerous to use and not many people understand it.

The importance of standardisation was emphasised in CCC: '*I think the worst thing that they can [do is to try] to de-standardize things… we have tried to standardize across the [organisation]. This is probably the same in every other organisation but particularly in CCC, everybody thinks that they are special, their division is special and therefore they should be doing it differently. I think that is the worst sin you can commit because unless you have really got a genuine reason – and I think there are very few – you should be going for the standardized approach as much as possible.*' The management accountants need to understand the data, analyse it and gain insights from it and then communicate that information to senior managers in such a way that they are first, alerted and second, can act on that data when they are ready to do so.

Management accountants should stop behaving as 'servants' and start educating and encouraging other functional staff to use the system to do their own analysis. A good example is overhead analysis. Management accountants should be encouraged to manage by exception rather than analysing minutiae and should focus on trends rather than absolutes. It was also suggested that they focus on providing support rather than control and providing information rather than data.

Perhaps most importantly, management accountants need to utilise the ERP system to free themselves to become business partners, leaving the generation of reports to the software. They need to participate in customer and business meetings, so learning more about their customers, while, at the same time, demonstrating what they do and how they can perform to the best advantage for the organisation.

7.1.2 Monitoring and Post-implementation Issues

Ongoing monitoring of the investment decision

In our cases, apart from CCC, no evidence was found that the other completed implementations were undertaking any formal ongoing monitoring of the investment decision. However, in each case (other than FFF which seemed likely to switch to another ERP system and, effectively abandon further development of their current system) where problems existed, steps were being taken to overcome them.

Ongoing monitoring of the impacts of the ERP system implementation

So far as monitoring the impacts of the ERP systems was concerned, an informal process appeared to be in place that was reactive in nature, rather than proactive.

That is, where problems surfaced, steps were taken to address them, but in few of the case study organisations was there any evidence that anyone was formally looking at the implementation and assessing the nature of the impact it was having on the people who were using it, or on the businesses processes.

The lack of continuous monitoring of the ERP system use we detected is short-sighted. It is well-known that technology must be used effectively if it is to positively impact individuals or processes. Further, the more IT is used, the more likely users will perceive that IT has an impact (either positive of negative) on their work. Such impacts might relate to task productivity, task innovation, management control, customer satisfaction, supplier management, etc. (Doll et al., 2003). By looking at how an implementation has impacted users, organisations can enhance their understanding of how their staff are reacting to it and can assess how they may react in the longer term to its use.

In the organisations we studied, managers are noticing the reactions of management accountants and other users to the ERP system. They are aware of what has worked and what has not, and of the impact that the implementation has had upon morale and working practices amongst the management accountants. However, little appears to be being done to bring less enthusiastic management accountants into line. They are being given the freedom to either leave the organisation (as was reported in some of the cases) or to do their jobs as they see best. In the more successful implementations, some management accountants are responding to this freedom by simply using the ERP system as a straight replacement for the previous legacy system: they use it to retrieve data which they import into other software and then produce the reports their customers want.

The organisations where this is happening are losing benefit that they could so easily gain if they were to implement effective education and support systems for the management accountants. Some, instead, are relying on natural wastage to remove the resistant management accountants, and have been successful in doing so. However, where the problem is significant, this is insufficient. All the organisations we studied need to put in place more effective education, training and support practices for the users of their ERP implementations. Until they do, even the best implementing organisations will gain less from the shift to ERP than they could. Models exist for identifying issues of this type that need to be addressed (see Doll et al., 2003) but, our interviewees all had a very clear idea of what was misaligned and had little need of models in pinpointing the issue.

Education

The education program used for any ERP implementation needs to recognise the differences in the knowledge of users, and the level of complexity in different functions. Users need two types of education, first they need to really understand what an ERP system is, and also how their role and actions affect everyone else who uses the system. Second, the users need 'hands-on' training of how to effectively and efficiently use the ERP system (Wallace and Kremzar, 2001).

New systems redefine job roles and thus create anxiety. Any information on the levels of training and promises to educate on an ongoing basis lessens resistance to change. The difficulties due to lack of proper training of users was one of the prime reasons behind the relatively unsuccessful ERP implementation at FFF. Organisations often provide scant attention to the education process, as this generally occurs at the end of the project which is generally over budget and behind schedule. This short-run view, as see within the reported cases, results in poor use and acceptance of the ERP system. Consequently, organisations have implemented ERP using a continuous improvement process (Ip et al., 2002) whereby they are forced into an iterative process for improving their ERP system.

Users must be given an appropriate introduction to the way the job is done, including training in use of the system and detailed instruction in the business processes and in how the system interacts with those processes. They need to know how what they do affects and is affected by the system. Once a group of users become familiar with the new system, they should take the role of mentor to teach others, including new entrants to the organisation who, irrespective of their prior experience and qualifications, will need time to become used to working with the system. Having untrained users using an ERP system is a recipe for errors and inefficiencies, as was demonstrated by the example given in Case G of the user who sent an invoice to a customer when he thought it was stored safely in his desk.

Alongside training, new performance standards and incentive programs need to be designed to align the interests of the organisation and its employees, so encouraging maximum buy-in to the benefits of using the system as opposed to continuing as much as possible to maintain old ways.

Assessing post-implementation benefits

Without an effective assessment of post-implementation benefits of the system, it is difficult to assess just how good a system is and whether project targets have been met. The consultant interviewed in Case B felt very strongly that management accountants were the appropriate users to construct post-implementation benefits tracking processes as part of the implementation, and that they should insist on one being included and upon being involved in its development.

Post-implementation review

Researchers have recommended evaluating the ERP project about 12–18 months after implementation to ensure that the promised benefits are actually attained

(Wallace and Kremzar, 2001; Powel and Barry, 2005). Post-implementation reviews can provide many benefits for an organisation, including the following:

- Identification of ways to improve the functional value of a project.
- Identification of ways and to assist users to overcome problems.
- Increased user morale through the continuous improvement of system environments.

In addition, undertaking a post-implementation review provides information and greater understanding of the system, its successful and unsuccessful aspects and its impacts (New South Wales Treasury, 2004).

Yet in the organisations that participated in this study, none seemed to have formally taken that evaluative step, if they did, the people we interviewed (and in each case we interviewed at least one member of the ERP project implementation team) were not aware of it. Most of the organisations we studied appeared to expect that the standard improvements claimed for ERP systems over traditional systems had or would arise and that the organisation would adjust to the new system in time. They simply expected that the implementation would be improved over time, so as to lead to greater positive benefits the longer the time period that elapsed since the system first went live.

Chapter 8

The Impact of ERP Systems on Management Accountants and Their Work

In all of these ERP implementations, whether successful or not, the management accountants were affected. The significance of the impact of the ERP system on the management accountants was related to the perceived success of the system implementation, with management accountants in the more successful organisations experiencing more dramatic changes. Even in organisations that were initially not very successful, there was a profound impact on the management accountants as their organisations learnt how to obtain more value out of the system. This indicates that as every organisation learns how to use the ERP system and obtain value from it, there will be a significant change in the role of the management accountants, the tasks performed by the management accountants and the skills required by the management accountants.

In this chapter, we consider these changes on the management accountants in the organisations we visited, looking at how the job of the management accountants evolved and the subsequent skills required for them to operate effectively in an ERP environment.

We conclude the chapter by providing a commentary on the impact of ERP systems in general on the work of management accountants.

8.1 The changing role of the management accountants

The extent to which the new system impacted upon the management accountants was assessed in relation to several aspects of their role:

1. Changes in time spent on data collection.
2. Changes in time spent on data analysis.
3. Changes in involvement in business decision-making.
4. Changes in focus on internal reporting.
5. Changes in focus on external environment.
6. Changes in focus from historic to forward-looking analysis.
7. Changes in focus from domain specific to cross-functional analysis.
8. Changes in use of time resulting from elimination of routine report generation.
9. Changes required in the management accountant's communication skills.
10. Changes in the formal and informal communication structure resulting from the ERP system.
11. Changes in the management accountant's job satisfaction resulting from the ERP system.

The first five aspects were scored by participants in the case studies on a scale from 1 to 7 (1: very much reduced to 7: very much increased). These scores are summarised in Table 8.1 and, along with the other six aspects, are discussed later. In order that comparisons may be made between the impact on their role and the level of success of the implementation, Table 8.1 also includes the perceived success of each implementation as shown previously in Table 4.2.

1. *Changes in Time Spent on Data Collection*

   All interviewees indicated that the management accountants spent significantly less time on data collection following the implementation of the ERP system irrespective

Table 8.1 The impact of the ERP systems on five aspects of the role of the management accountants

Criteria	AAA	BBB	CCC	DDD	EEE	GGG
1. Time spent on data collection	2	2	1	3	1	2
2. Time spent on data analysis	6	4	6	5	2	4
3. Involvement in business decision-making	6	5	7	4	7	5
4. Focus on internal reporting	5	4	6	7	6	2
5. Focus on external environment	n/a	5	7	5	2	7
Success (from Table 4.2)	3	3	3	2	2	1

The scores relate to: 'On a scale from 1 to 7 (1: very much reduced to 7: very much increased).' The success scores from Table 4.2: Significant 3; Moderate 2; Not significant 1.
Note: FFF did not participate in this set of questions.

of whether the implementation was a success or not. There was also an indication that the type of data collected had changed. For example, EEE indicated that the manual accruals had decreased considerably since implementation of the ERP system.

2. *Changes in Time Spent on Data Analysis*

Most interviewees indicated that management accountants are spending a lot more time on data analysis.

3. *Changes in Involvement in Business Decision-Making*

All respondents agreed that management accountants were more involved in business decision-making following the implementation of the ERP system.

4. *Changes in Focus on Internal Reporting*

The focus of the management accountants on internal reporting (e.g. performance measures and control issues) increased in all companies except GGG (which was a less than successful implementation) where it was considered to have decreased.

5. *Changes in Focus on External Environment*

Where it was applicable to the company, the focus of the management accountants on the external environment (e.g. benchmarking) had increased.

6. *Changes in Focus from Historic to Forward-Looking Analysis*

In all the organisations that had a successful implementation, the management accountants are involved in significantly more forward-looking analyses. This is most likely a result of the capability of the ERP systems to generate virtually any desired historical-based report. As such, there is limited need for the management accountants to perform the mundane data gathering and reporting of historic-based reports. The management accountants are spending much more time and effort on business planning.

Although the percentage change varies by company (and also depends upon the relative percentages prior to the implementation), the average change ranges from over 50% to 80–85% more forward-looking analyses. Historic data is now being used more to forecast what is going to happen and the concern is with future success rather than looking at detail into the past.

There are a variety of reasons for the change in focus. Prior to the ERP system implementation, the management accountants needed to track down the needed data, organise it and then present it to the management. With the implementation of the ERP system, the historic data is automatically captured and presented to managers in a format that can be used immediately. In a successful implementation, there is more trust in the data within the new system. An ERP system also makes it a lot easier to perform forward-looking analysis. Finally, the managers in organisations with successful ERP implementations are demanding more forward-looking analyses from the management accountants.

Clearly, the role of management accountants will change when an ERP system is implemented, the management accountant will be providing more information for planning and guiding the organisation, rather than providing backward-looking reports telling the organisation where it had been.

7. *Changes in Focus from Domain Specific to Cross-Functional Analysis*

The implementation of ERP systems is viewed as a prerequisite for cross-functional analysis for most of these organisations. In virtually every instance, prior to the implementation of the ERP system, the data wasn't available to undertake cross-functional analysis. Now that the data is available, the management accountants are involved in cross-functional analysis. The ERP system captures and provides the data on third-party contractors, procurement issues, maintenance costs, asset management and other areas – data which is difficult to capture in a non-ERP environment. The management accountants are now able to take that data and identify how much a project will cost and the relative profitability across the entire businesses, something that was previously impracticable.

This change in focus to more cross-functional analysis occurred even if management accounting is organised on a functional basis. Management accounting is moving towards cross-functional business process analysis from domain specific analysis. Several interviewees expected that this change will develop further over several years.

The inherent capability of the ERP system in more successful implementations is viewed as an enabler of cross-sectional analysis. The reorganisation of the data and implementation of a single chart of accounts across all the business units resulting from the ERP system implementation helped foster the growth of cross-functional analysis: *'There is so much more cross-functional stuff now. That was one of our frustrations with the old system particularly when you had 36 General Ledger [systems] and you could hardly do anything across the whole [organisation], or even across your divisions in some instances'* (Case C). Other organisations used the ERP implementation to enable the development and implementation of a data warehouse. The data warehouse was viewed as critical for the significant cross-functional analysis that the management accountants are now able to perform.

Even if there is still a significant amount of functional analysis, the organisations believe that the big difference is the ability to see 'end-to-end' business processes, and to have more depth in the data. This is a result of increased information visibility, an outcome that is often associated with ERP systems.

However, in the organisations that had a less successful ERP implementation, such as GGG, there is little change in the amount of cross-functional analysis. Unfortunately, this makes intuitive sense. The management accountants are still trying to provide the same type of information from the system as the managers were using prior to the ERP implementation. Since the management accountants must provide the 'old style' reports, there is no time for cross-functional analysis. Thus the level of success of the implementation had a direct bearing on whether or not this aspect of the role of the management accountants changed.

8. *Changes in Use of Time Resulting From Elimination of Routine Report Generation*

The more successful ERP system implementations resulted in other changes in how the management accountants use their time. The ERP system, in general, is able to generate all of the routine management reports. Since these reports were previously the responsibility of the management accountants, they now have more time available to complete other tasks. In most organisations, this release of time has resulted in a change in how the management accountants approach their job, and in how the management accountants are perceived by others in the organisation. In general, the management accountants are now supporting the business and decision-making with improved forecasts and strategic planning, writing proposals and analysis. In some settings, the management accountant is becoming more of a business partner to senior management.

The management accountants are interacting more with other functional areas of the business. *'The Management Accountants are spending a lot of time attending customer meetings and actually dealing with customers. They provide "a reality check" to the promises made by the Sales team. They provide the business unit heads with forecasts of activity in the next 3 months – forecasts are vital to the business when there are approximately 6,000 projects. Before the implementation of the new system, it was very difficult to manage 6,000 projects. The Management Accountants are now... on top of the projects'* (Case A).

The extra time is also reflected in a lower level of stress experienced by management accountants at the month-end. *'This is the kind of work that they do now and it is very much not an end-of-month exercise anymore. Whereas before [the implementation of the new system], it was always getting everything together so that we can report it at the end of the month. Now on a daily basis, they are looking at what is happening in the business. It is a massive change for them and it has taken them away from the old fashioned financial everybody works hard at the month-end, and comes in on a Saturday and Sunday, and then rushing around to try and get ready for the next month-end'* (Case A).

In some organisations, the extra time is spent performing more sensitivity 'what next' type of analysis. This also reflects a stronger role for the management accountant of business partner to management. These analyses provided by the management accountant attempt to move the business from its current operations to where it needs to be in the future, from both a financial and business strategy perspective. They generally include going beyond financial analysis to controls, and whether the business is getting where it needs to be from a control perspective, including the metrics to use to measure the controls.

The more successful ERP implementations have therefore allowed the management accountants more time for different, more value-added data analysis. The management accountants are becoming business partners to top management – they are out meeting with their customers and establishing stronger working relationships with them, with obvious benefits to both sides.

However, where the implementation was less successful, there really is no extra time being generated because the management accountants must first identify the problem and then obtain the correct data. *'They are probably spending more time sorting out the problems than they used to because they didn't have these problems before. You [now] know all the projects that have been set up incorrectly so they are going into the wrong area of their accounts or they are being traded in an incorrect manner, or something'* (Case G). The management accountants in less successful implementations, therefore, find themselves in the unenviable position of actually having less time available to complete 'normal' tasks, as they now need to identify and fix problems introduced by the poor ERP implementation.

9. *Changes Required in the Management Accountant's Communication Skills*

The focus is now much more on 'what the data means' and 'where the organisation can go.' Prior to the implementation of the ERP system, communication was primarily concerned with reviewing what happened. As a result, all participants believed that communication skills are more important in an ERP environment. Management accountants need to be able to interpret and provide the information to the users in a manner that the managers understand – they need to be technically competent, and they must be able to communicate their findings.

Although communication was always important, a higher level of communication skills is required in an ERP environment because management accountants are now not only looking at other aspects of the data, they are also far more involved in discussions with the senior business management team. In order to be business partners, management accountants must provide insight and present the information at the time and in the manner that the manager needs that information to make a decision. The ability to know what information to present, and when and how to present it, is a specific skill that management accountants need to be far better at in an ERP environment.

10. *Changes in the Formal and Informal Communication Structure Resulting from the ERP System*

No link was found between the implementation of the ERP system and the changes in the formal and informal communication structure. By its very nature, an ERP system results in significant centralisation of data. This is often associated with a more formal communication structure. However, the cases revealed that the existing organisational structure and culture have a greater impact on the communication structure than the ERP system. '*Whether it is more formal or not is difficult to say, I think it is a company culture thing rather than a management accountant thing. We are in a fast moving industry, things change so rapidly a lot of what we do is informal*' (Case A). '*CCC is quite an informal organisation culturally. [We] are not greatly into formality in any way, shape, or form*' (Case C). However, there was an indication of frustration in some organisations because ERP systems foster and embody a centralised structure which, at times, ran counter to the informal organisation culture.

11. *Changes in the Management Accountant's Job Satisfaction Resulting From the ERP System*

The ERP system implementations generally resulted in increased job satisfaction for the management accountants (or at least the management accountants who remained at the organisation after the ERP system was implemented). Job satisfaction needs to be examined over a period of time, rather than at a specific point in time. If asked immediately after the ERP system was implemented, most management accountants would have been very frustrated with the software, the hours, the task and most everything else. After the system was operating for a longer period of time (usually at least 6 months), the level of job satisfaction would be significantly higher. This was very apparent in Case G. After the system was operational for a period of time, the management accountant has learnt the software, knows what data is available and has seen how the job is evolving from putting historic numbers together to becoming a business partner to top managers.

A number of the organisations experienced a reduction in staff turnover after the implementation of the ERP system. Rather than having a member of staff leave on average every 6 months, no turnover was reported over the past 3 years in Case A. There is, however, some self-selection made by the management accountants. In Case D, the organisation reported that several management accountants left because they were just tired, that they just had enough, whereas the management accountants who were subsequently hired are satisfied with the environment.

8.2 Skills needed by management accountants in ERP environments

The changes identified in the role of management accountants in an ERP environment mean that they need a slightly different set of skills than the skills that were sufficient in a non-ERP environment. The most significant change appears to relate to understanding the business and business processes, and to be able to communicate the analyses to management as a business partner. The participants in this research were very consistent in their perception of the skills needed by management accountants in ERP environments. All of the interviewees started from the perspective that the management accountant has both appropriate and adequate accounting training. Some believed that a formal accounting qualification was very desirable as a way to signal that a management accountant possesses the requisite skills. What almost every participant identified was the need for good communication and interpersonal skills. Analytical skills and the ability to focus on objectives, prioritise work (work management) were also deemed important. The following quote from Case B best summarises this point.

> 'To me, the skills... however you define skills, competencies, whatever... the critical ones that I would be looking for are more behavioural, interpersonal, etc. ... I would tend to take it as read that if somebody was a qualified Management Accountant... they'd have appropriate analytical, numeracy, etc. skills and [They are] going to be working in an Accounting Department but [they are] going to be involved in everything... I have met and worked with lots of accountants and have noticed that, in reality, often the less successful ones are those with the poorest interpersonal skills. Unfortunately, when

organisations recruit accountants they focus on qualifications and technical experience and rarely focus on interpersonal or behavioural skills I feel very strongly that an accountant's ability to relate and work effectively with non-accountants and other functional specialists is imperative, especially in an ERP environment where all the systems and processes are integrated and therefore inter-dependent.'

The increased importance in understanding the business was also emphasised, as was the need to have 'entrepreneurial salesman skills.' That is, the management accountants need to be able to communicate with the management team and synthesise and explain the results (the impact of the financial data) in a way that can be easily understood. Management accountants need to take on a partnership role with the managers. This will sometimes result in the management accountants supporting major decisions by influencing managers onto the right area through a thoughtful and reasoned explanation of what the information means.

Another interview neatly summarised the need for a different set of skills: *'There is a danger when you have a new system that there is so much information (and one of the things that I have said is good about our SAP implementation is the fact that you can get loads more information out) they need the analysis ability but, together with that, they need the decision-making ability to decide what is important and what isn't important; because I think that there [is] a danger to start with that you could just get overwhelmed with the [amount of] data coming at you and they [have] to be able to prioritise what [is] the stuff we really [need] to look at and what we [don't] need to look at. The other thing I think they [need is] really good planning skills, both day-to-day planning skills and also turning those into the ability to do longer term budgeting and forecasting.'*

The skill set identified by the participants in this study is summarised in Table 8.2. In this table we organise the skills according to general categories (e.g. communication, leadership, technical, etc.).

In addition to describing new or enhanced existing skills that are needed in an ERP environment, participants identified skills that are *less* relevant in an ERP environment. These included the 'traditional number crunching skill' – the ERP system can produce those numbers (faster and likely more accurately). Nevertheless, management accountants need to be able to interpret those numbers, understand how those numbers were produced and provide insight.

The changes in the skills required for management accountants working in an ERP environment have more to do with emphasis than with a completely new set of attributes they must acquire, though there are some obvious exceptions, such as the need to provide leadership and to work in partnership *with* management rather than *for* management. However, even changes in emphasis can be daunting, particularly when they occur 'overnight' on rollout day. This may provide some explanation for

Table 8.2 Skills needed by management accountants in ERP environments

Good communication skills, including:
- Ability to explain the analysis to get to allow the manager to understand the issue and take action
- Presentation skills
- Good interpersonal skills
- Influence and persuasion skills
- Entrepreneurial salesman skills
- Ability to work effectively with non-accountants

Leadership, decision-making, analytical and planning skills, including:
- Support the making of big decisions, influencing managers onto the right ground
- Good analytical skills, need to know what you are looking for and need the ability to find out on your own to know what questions to ask to get somebody else to find it
- Partnership role with managers
- A combination of being able to get into the big picture and synthesise
- Be able to spot things that are wrong and have an idea of how to fix them
- Ability to focus on objectives, work management
- Planning skills – time management, both short-term and long-term
- Change management skills
- Manage and hold others accountable for decisions
- Ability to prioritise

Technical skills, including:
- Depending on their role in the team, technical skills and good software skills (with the ability to adapt)
- Numeracy skills
- Software skills
- IT skills
- Ability to learn quickly

Business understanding, including:
- Understand business processes
- Be able to relate to what the business is about

Educator skills, including:
- Educating the customer to the way management accountants provide value
- Be able to explain how the numbers were obtained and what they mean and be able to explain how the system generates those numbers

General skills, including:
- Patience – ERP systems can be difficult to use at first
- Integrity

the turnover of management accountants in organisations that successfully implemented an ERP system. In those organisations, the management accountants who liked the 'old' way of doing things (i.e. the number crunching) would no longer have the job they previously enjoyed. In fact, they would now need to provide insights and deal with various levels of managers rather than other accountants. Not surprisingly, these tended to be the management accountants who moved elsewhere, and they were replaced by management accountants who had an affinity with the different role required of them in an ERP environment.

8.3 General impact of ERP systems on the work of management accountants

ERP systems have the ability to provide for consistency in the application of business rules. Once the business process is defined and implemented within the ERP system, that process will be followed and any deviations will be tracked. This increased compliance with management policies and procedures provides significant benefits for both internal auditors and management accountants. This is very important in a world in which compliance issues (e.g. IFRS, Basel II, SOX, etc.) are of paramount concern for the finance director and other company directors. This is where the management accountants must both provide the advice needed to successfully implement the controls and ensure that the correct data is both captured and able to be reported in a meaningful manner. Further, the management accountants must resist the temptation to simply pull the raw data from the ERP system and toss it about in a spreadsheet.

For example, although the Sarbanes–Oxley (SOX) Act of 2002 only directly applies to publicly traded companies in the USA, its impact is widely felt throughout the global economy. Many private companies are implementing parts of it as long as they are able to identify sound business reasons and quantifiable benefits (Reed et al., 2005). Further, many lenders are asking private companies about their internal controls as a direct result of SOX (Heffes, 2005).

Within this environment, the management accountant needs to work with both internal audit and the IT staff to help create the business case for implementing aspects of SOX. In the context of this research project and also based upon other articles (e.g. Van Decker, 2007) one common failing we encountered in all the cases is the loss of controls during the consolidation process. There is an over-dependence on spreadsheets which history has shown often results in the introduction of errors. A financial consolidation solution based upon the ERP system could be used to improve compliance with SOX and automate the organisation's financial consolidation processes. This is just one area in which the management accountant can make a difference. The same holds true for IFRS reporting. Again, the reporting, from a control/compliance perspective should be incorporated into the ERP system, just like the consolidation process. The management accountants, in the organisations which have implemented ERP systems, have the opportunity to provide advice and be the conduit between top management and the IT staff. Again, this was an element sadly missing in the organisations we visited.

The role of the management accountant changed dramatically with the implementation of some of the ERP systems, from gathering data from multiple sources and creating spreadsheets reporting historical results, to proactive participation in the managerial planning and control process using historic and planning data from the ERP system. However, this occurred only in the successful organisations. Nonetheless, there are many tasks of this type that management accountants can perform even if their organisation has not implemented an ERP system (or is still in the implementation process).

One area of concern is that of outsourced ERP (and other) systems. This is especially true as more vendors provide both a 'software as a service' model and other, more traditional outsourced approaches. There is a significant need for the management accountant to be more involved in cross-functional analysis. The traditional issues related to ERP implementation and use still exist. However, the management accountant needs to be involved in the evaluation of the contract during the negotiation process and also in the evaluation as to whether the promised value is actually received from the vendor.

There was evidence provided in the interviews that management accountants are increasingly involved in cross-functional analysis. Further, management accountants now examine project timelines, profitability of projects and perform an appraisal of projects rather than just generating the numbers. They help generate ROI calculations and help ensure that the total cost of ownership stays within predetermined ranges. They monitor projects and recommend appropriate action rather than simply gathering data and not knowing the outcome until after the project is finished. This includes analyses of third-party contractors, procurement, maintenance, asset management and elsewhere. They provide projections of what/how the organisation will benefit from the contractual agreements.

Within the context of the development of ERP systems and the enterprise data models, which are the basis for the enterprise systems, it has been suggested that the data models be built in order to achieve compliance with various standards, for example ISO 9001 (Kim et al., 2007). As a subject matter expert, the management accountant should be involved in the data model development. They understand the business and also understand the regulatory environment to which the organisation is accountable. As shown in this research, and consistent with published research, the involvement of subject matter experts early in a project results in higher levels of success than late or non-involvement.

Another area that has seen increased emphasis, especially in light of various government mandates resulting from identity theft and similar concerns is that of data stewardship. Organisations are realising that they are not the true owners of data (e.g. the customer owns their own data). Instead, they are the stewards of the data and as such must provide due diligence and act with care with respect to that data. There are multiple facets to this endeavour. One is the establishment of a data quality management programme. This programme combines both business and technical perspectives for creating high quality strategic and operational data (Wende, 2007). Although the management accountant would likely not be the organisational data steward, it is likely that the management accountant is a subject area data steward (Newman and Logan, 2006). Organisations need a data governance framework which allows them to respond to strategic and operational challenges (Wende, 2007). The management accountant could play an important role in this process as a business steward who understands the business need and can assess the impact of new business requirements on data quality/stewardship, or more likely during the establishment phase of data stewardship on business processes and requirements.

The role of the management accountants within the organisations we studied that have successfully implemented ERP systems has changed dramatically. The role has evolved to that of a true business partner who is helping to interpret data and provide guidance for strategic and tactical plans. These management accountants are no longer gathering data from disparate systems and reporting on what happened 3 weeks ago, and which accounts are in arrears. Most, if not all of the standard operational reports are available at the touch of a button, prepared without the need to call on the management accountant. This is a wonderful situation for the profession, and one that ought to be embraced rather than, as we saw in our case studies, pushed to one side by some management accountants who prefer to stick with their old ways.

There are also additional challenges. In those organisations where there have been less successful ERP implementations, the management accountant is often overworked, needing to verify the data coming from the ERP system and provide the same reports as before, while trying to provide some forward-looking information that is now accessible following the ERP implementation.

More generally, what management accountants can achieve following successful ERP implementations affects the management accountant of tomorrow. We have already seen that they will likely be called upon to provide oversight in a number of relatively new areas, irrespective of whether an ERP system has been implemented. Key areas include the evaluation and control of outsourcing and software as a service agreement. In addition, data modelling, data quality and data stewardship are areas in which the management accountant must participate. The management accountant is a subject matter expert who can provide insight into organisation business processes and also help identify areas of concern.

Summary and Conclusions

Chapter 9

This project has resulted in numerous rich insights that are critical for understanding the way the role of management accountants in an ERP environment differs from their role in a conventional non-ERP environment. One of the most striking insights is in the differential effect on the management accountant of successful compared to less successful ERP implementations.

Interviewees, all of whom have been through an ERP system implementation, have provided invaluable advice for management accountants in practice and for CIMA members in general. This advice is generally consistent with that reported in the literature (e.g. Granlund and Malmi, 2002; Caglio, 2003; Lodh and Gaffikin,

2003; Quattrone and Hopper, 2003; Scapens and Jazayeri, 2003; Rom and Rohde, 2004). The outcomes obtained by the organisations in this study is consistent with the literature which reports that only about 15% of the firms are initially satisfied with the performance improvements from the ERP systems (James and Wolf, 2000).

In all seven case studies, the role of the management accountants was affected. The significance of the impact of the ERP system on the role of the management accountant was related to the success of the system implementation. The more successful implementations resulted in dramatic changes to the nature of their role whereby the management accountant became a business advisor who took proactive steps to aid the various executives and decision-makers. In the less successful implementations there was a dysfunctional impact upon the management accountants even where the tasks they were expected to perform had not changed.

These findings support our decision, taken after looking at the literature in this area, to include the success of the ERP implementation in Granlund and Malmi's (2002) model. We therefore include this in the revised model presented in Figure 9.1.

Of particular relevance to CIMA members and other management accountants in practice, not only was much evidence of change in the role of the management accountant found in this study, redundancies within the management accounting function were also reported – in Case D, for example, management intend to reduce the number of management accountants by 40% when the project revisions are completed. Management accountants in an ERP environment need to be business partners and confidantes of the other managers in the organisation. They need a strong understanding of the business (business processes), significant interpersonal

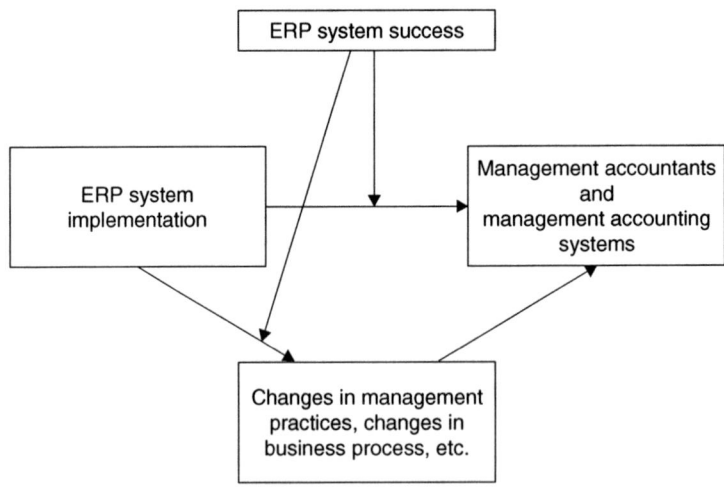

Figure 9.1 Impact of ERP systems on management accountants and management accounting. *Source*: Adapted from Granlund and Malmi (2002).

skills, leadership skills, decision-making skills, analytical skills, planning skills and technical skills (including computer and accounting), in all cases, at higher levels than in a non-ERP environment. Management accountants who do not possess these skills at an appropriate level will join the ranks of those reported in the cases who were made redundant or left voluntarily. Organisations which implement an ERP system are demanding value and a return on everything, including their employees.

Time, scope and budget control are very important to successful projects, none more so than when ERP implementations are involved. More importantly, external factors outside the scope of the project team also play a role in determining the success or failure of a project. However, if the project team is appropriately selected, the project implementation plan is properly designed, the issues are clearly communicated and the process is meticulously executed with appropriate support; organisations will have a better likelihood of overcoming process-and-technology-related issues to deliver the project with minimal problems.

It was found to be critical in our study that management accountants be involved in ERP implementations from the start, that they are recognised as key members of the project team and that they champion the change process. Where this was not the case, projects were less successful and the management accountants found their role considerably less manageable as a result. Additionally, in projects that were initially less than successful, and the management accountants became involved during the rework stage, the resultant projects were subsequently viewed as more successful. Even in these situations, the management accountants found their tasks to be dramatically changed. Users' involvement and, in this particular context, the involvement of the management accountants in the ERP implementation was critical (see Cameron and Meyer, 1998; Clemons, 1998). Involving all user types in the project enables the project team to be aware of users' requirements and address their concerns (Best, 1997).

We found that it is critical that management accountants be proactive in seeking involvement in ERP implementation projects, not just for the sake of the organisation, but for their own benefit, and that if they were not involved initially, they can still bring similar results through their subsequent involvement when the system is reworked. This is consistent with prior research, not just through the positive education impact upon them if they are involved in development (they learn about the systems and the new business processes), but also because managerial skills of communication and team building are among the most important in an ERP implementation (Appleton, 1999) and they are likely to improve their own communication skills through involvement in project development as they need to learn how to communicate their tasks and needs to others in the team who know nothing about management accounting.

The key to managing change – be it in process or technology – remains in tackling the 'people' issues: establishing a common goal and working together with primary users – that is why management accountants in the relatively more successful ERP implementations have higher levels of job satisfaction and lower levels of staff turnover. Organisations that fail to achieve expected performance improvements through ERP projects do not have effective change management capabilities (Lee and Lee, 2004). When an organisation moves to a complex ERP environment, changes in staff relationships generally occur and employees will likely need to acquire new skills, assume additional responsibilities, create new working relationships and share information among departments (Appleton, 1999). This was very evident in our findings. Successful ERP implementations required a change in the skill set possessed by management accountants. They needed to become more analytical and forward-looking, and they needed greater interpersonal communication and presentation skills, rather than continuing with the traditional skill set of data gatherer, number cruncher and report producer with basic analytical skills.

It is clear that the role of management accountants in an ERP environment is more like a business advisor to top management than that of a traditional management accountant. CIMA needs to acknowledge this and encourage its membership towards reskilling itself to meet this challenge and its members need to take heed of this and take note of the warnings described in this chapter if they continue to be held in the regard that they currently enjoy. ERP systems are currently the software tool of the largest organisations, but many medium-sized organisations are also moving in this direction. It will not be too far into the future before an ERP approach is the norm across all organisations.

References

Akkermans, H. and van Helden, K. (2002), Vicious and virtuous cycles in ERP implementation: A case study of interrelations between success factors. *European Journal of Information Systems*, 11(1): 35–46.

Aloini, D., Dulmin, R. and Mininno, V. (2007), Risk management in ERP project introduction: Review of the literature. *Information and Management*, 44(6): 547–567.

Appleton, E. (1999), How to survive ERP. *Datamation*, March.

Best, C. (1997), Integrated system builds on human foundation. *Computing Canada*: (23).

Booth, P., Matolcsy, Z. and Wieder, B. (2000), Integrated information systems (ERP-systems) and accounting practice – The Australian experience. *Third European Conference on Accounting Information Systems*, Munich, Germany.

Brignall, S. and Ballantine, J. (2004), Strategic enterprise management systems: New directions for research. *Management Accounting Review*, 15: 22–240.

Caglio, A. (2003), Enterprise resource planning systems and accountants: Towards hybridization? *European Accounting Review*, 12 (1): 123–153.

Cameron, D.P. and Meyer, L.S. (1998), Rapid ERP implementation – A contradiction. *Management Accounting (USA)*, 80.

Carr, N.G. (2003), IT doesn't matter. *Harvard Business Review*, May: 41–49.

Clemons, C. (1998), Successful implementation of an enterprise system: A case study. *Proceedings of the AIS Conference Americans*, Baltimore, MD: 109–110.

Cullen, J., Bernon, M., Tsamenyi, M. and Gorst, J. (2007), Reverse logistics in the UK retail sector: A case study of the role of ERP systems and management accounting in driving organisational change. *Working paper: University of Warwick*, 28 November.

Davenport, T.H. (1998), Putting the enterprise into the enterprise system. *Harvard Business Review*, 76 (4): 121–133.

Davenport, T.H. (2000), *Mission Critical: Realizing the Promise of Enterprise Systems*. Boston, MA: Harvard Business School Press.

Deutsch, C.H. (1998), Software that can make a grown company cry. *The New York Times*, November 8.

Doll, W.J., Deng, X. and Scazzero, J.A. (2003), A process for post-implementation IT benchmarking. *Information and Management*, 41 (2): 199–212.

Edwards, J.B. (2001), ERP, balanced scorecard, and IT: How do they fit together? *Journal of Corporate Accounting and Finance*, 12(5): 3–12.

Eisenhardt, K.M. (1985), Control: Organizational and economic approaches. *Management Science*, 31 (2): 134–149.

Eisenhardt, K.M. (1989), Agency theory: An assessment and review. *Academy of Management Review*, 14(1): 57–74.

ERP-SELECT. (2004), *The top 12 reasons ERP projects fail*. Available at http://erp.ittoolbox.com/groups/vendor-selection/erp-select/eraselect-erp-for-university-587056 on 14 April 2008.

Fahy, M.J. (2000), Strategic enterprise management: The implications for management accounting and control. *23rd Annual Congress, European Accounting Association*, (March), Munich, Germany.

Fearon, C. (2000), The budgeting nightmare. *CMA Management*, May: 11–12.

Gould, S. (2003), *Improving decision making in your organisation: The CIMA strategic enterprise management (SEM) initiative*. Available at www.cimaglobal.com/cps/rde/xbcr/SID-0AAAC564-11FF9E29/live/sem_techrpt_2003.pdf). London: CIMA.

Grabski, S.V. and Leech, S. (2007), Complementary controls and ERP implementation success. *International Journal of Accounting Information Systems*, 8(1): 17–39.

Grabski, S.V., Leech, S.A. and Lu, B. (2001), Risks and controls in the implementation of ERP systems. *International Journal of Digital Accounting Research*, 1(1): 51–78.

Granlund, M. and Malmi, T. (2002), Moderate impact of ERPS on management accounting: A lag or permanent outcome? *Management Accounting Research*, 13: 299–321.

Granlund, M. and Mouritsen, J. (2003), Introduction: Problematizing the relationship between management accounting and information technology. *European Accounting Review*, 12(1): 77–83.

Heffes, E.M. (2005), FEI CEO's 2005 Top 10 Financial Reporting Issues. *Financial Executive*, 21(1): 17.

Holland, C.P. and Light, B. (1999), A critical success factors model for ERP implementation. *IEEE Software*, 16(3): 30–36.

Hong, K.-K. and Kim, Y.-G. (2002), The critical success factors for ERP implementation: An organisational fit perspective. *Information and Management*, 40(1): 25–40.

Hunton, J.E., Lippincott, B. and Reck, J.L. (2003), Enterprise resource planning systems: Comparing firm performance of adopters and nonadopters. *International Journal of Accounting Information Systems*, 4(3): 165–184.

Hyvonen, T. (2003), Management accounting and information systems: ERP versus BoB. *European Accounting Review*, 12(1): 155–173.

Ip, W.H., Chau, K.Y. and Chan, S.F. (2002), Implementing ERP through continuous improvement. *International Journal of Manufacturing Technology and Management*, 4(6): 465–479.

James, D. and Wolf, M.L. (2000), A second wind for ERP. *The McKinsey Quarterly* (2): 100–107.

Jarrar, Y.F., Al-Mudimigh, A. and Zairi, M. (2000), ERP implementation critical success factors–The role and impact of business process management. *Proceedings of the 2000 IEEE International Conference on Management of Innovation and Technology, ICMIT 2000*, 1:122–127.

Kim, H.M., Fox, M.S. and Sengupta, A. (2007), How to build enterprise data models to achieve compliance to standards or regulatory requirements (and share data). *Journal of the Association for Information Systems*, 8(2): 105–128.

Kirsch, L.J. (1996), The management of complex tasks in organizations: Controlling the systems development process. *Organizational Science*, 7(1): 1–21.

Kirsch, L.J. (1997), Portfolios of control modes and IS project management. *Information Systems Research*, 8 (3): 215–239.

Kirsch, L.J., Sambamurthy, V., Ko, D-G. and Purvis, R.L. (2002), Controlling information systems development projects: The view from the client. *Management Science*, 48 (4): 484–498.

Latamore, G. (1999), Flexibility fuels the ERP evolution. *APICS – The Performance Advantage*, October: 44–50.

Lee, S.C. and Lee, H.G. (2004), The importance of change management after ERP implementation: An information capability perspective. *Proceedings of the Twenty-Fifth International Conference on Information Systems*, Las Vegas, NV, December 11–14: 939–953.

Lodh, S.C. and Gaffikin, M.J.R. (2003), Implementation of an integrated accounting and cost management system using the SAP system: A field study. *European Accounting Review*, 12(1): 85–121.

Lucas, H.C., Walton, E.J. and Ginzberg, M.J. (1988), Implementing packaged software. *MIS Quarterly*: 537–549.

Maccarone, P. (2000), The impact of ERPs on management accounting and control systems and the changing role of controllers. *EAA 23rd Annual Congress*, Munich, Germany, 29–31 March.

Manufacturing Business Technology (2008), IDC: Mid-market ERP penetration in Latin America to grow 27%. *Business News Americas – English*, April 8. Tuesday 4:09 PM GMT http://www.mbtmag.com/articleXml/LN772386882.html

Milgrom, P. and Roberts, J. (1990), The economics of modern manufacturing: Technology, strategy and organization. *American Economic Review*, 80: 511–528.

Milgrom, P. and Roberts, J. (1994), Comparing equilibria. *American Economic Review*, 84: 441–459.

Milgrom, P. and Roberts, J. (1995), Complementarities and fit: Strategy, structure, and organizational change in manufacturing. *Journal of Accounting and Economics*, 19: 179–208.

New South Wales Treasury (2004), *Total asset management: Post implementation review guideline.* Sydney, Australia: New South Wales Treasury.

Newman, D. and Logan, D. (2006), *Governance is an Essential Building Block for Enterprise Information Management.* Stamford, CT: Gartner Research.

Olhager, J. and Selldin, E. (2003), Enterprise resource planning survey of Swedish manufacturing firms. *European Journal of Operational Research*, 146(2): 365–373.

Ouchi, W.G. (1979), A conceptual framework for the design of organizational control mechanisms. *Management Science*, 25(9): 833–848.

Poston, R. and Grabski, S. (2001), Financial impacts of enterprise resource planning implementations. *International Journal of Accounting Information Systems*, 2(4): 271–294.

Powel, W.D. and Barry, J. (2005), An ERP post-implementation review: Planning for the future by looking back. *Educause Quarterly*, 3: 40–46.

Quattrone, P. and Hopper, T. (2003), *Management control systems in multinational organisations: The effects of implementing ERP.* Briefing 09.03. London: ICAEW.

Reed, R.O., Sinnett, W.M., Buchman, T. and Wobbekind, R. (2005), Why should private companies implement Sarbanes–Oxley?. *Financial Executive*, 21(3): 54–57.

Rom, A. and Rohde, C. (2004), Integrated information systems (IIS) and management accounting: Evidence from the Danish Practice. *First International Conference on Enterprise Systems and Accounting*, Thessaloniki, Greece, 3–4 September.

Scapens, R.W. and Jazayeri, M. (2003), ERP systems and management accounting change: Opportunities or impacts? A research note. *European Accounting Review*, 12(1): 201–233.

Scott, J. (1999), The FoxMeyer drugs' bankruptcy: Was it a failure of ERP? *Proceedings of AMCIS 1999 Americas Conference on Information Systems*: 223–225.

Somers, T. and Nelson, K.G. (2001), The impact of critical success factors across stages of enterprise resource planning implementations. *Proceedings of the 34th Hawaii International Conference on Systems Science,* January 3–6, Maui, Hawaii.

Turnick, P.A. (1999), ERP: Promise or pipe dream? *Transportation & Distribution*, 40(1): 23–26.

Van Decker, J.E. (2007), Improving SOX compliance sustainability with financial consolidation applications. *Gartner Report #G00145589*. February.

Wallace, T.F. and Kremzar, M.H. (2001), *ERP: Making it happen: The implementers' guide to success with enterprise resource planning.* John Wiley & Sons.

Wende, K. (2007), A model for data governance – Organising accountabilities for data quality management. *Eighteen Australasian Conference on Information Systems*, Toowoomba, 5–7 December: 417–425.

Yusuf, Y., Gunasekaran, A. and Abthorpe, M.S. (2004), Enterprise information systems project implementation: A case study of ERP in Rolls-Royce. *International Journal of Production Economics*, 87: 251–266.

Appendices

Appendix 1

Case Studies Summary

The seven companies interviewed gradually moved to using an enterprise resource planning system over the last 7 years. Both the stage of completion and the relative success of the ERP implementation varied across the companies, as did the length of time required to implement the ERP system. However, in all cases, there is a strong association between the perceived success of the ERP system and the involvement of management accountants in the ERP implementation.

Regardless of the level of success of the ERP implementation, the role of the management accountants was affected. However, the significance of the impact of the ERP system on the role of the management accountant was related to the perceived success of the system implementation, with those in more successful organisations experiencing the more dramatic changes.

All interviewees agreed that management accountants spent significantly less time on data collection following the implementation of the ERP system irrespective of whether the implementation was a success or not. Most agreed that management accountants were spending a lot more time on data analysis. All agreed that management accountants were more involved in business decision-making, especially in more successful implementations. The focus of the management accountants on internal reporting increased in most cases, whereas the focus on the external environment increased where it was applicable to the business.

In all three organisations that had a successful implementation, the management accountants are involved in significantly more forward-looking analyses than previously. In organisations in which the ERP implementation was less successful, the management accountants still spend a significant amount of time on generating historic reports, although some change to more forward-looking analysis was indicated.

The implementation of ERP systems was viewed as a prerequisite for cross-functional analysis for almost all the organisations. This change is occurring even if management accounting is organised on a functional basis, although several organisations expected that this change will occur gradually over several years. Once again, this change was most pronounced in those organisations that had a more successful implementation.

The more successful ERP system implementations resulted in other changes in how the management accountants use their time. Since the ERP system is able to generate routine management reports, the management accountants are now expected to support the business and decision-making with improved forecasts and strategic planning; becoming more of a business partner to senior management and involved more with customers. In less-than-successful implementations, the management accountants are in the unenviable position of actually having less time available to complete 'normal' tasks as they are having to spend time identifying problems arising from the system and trying to obtain the correct data.

In general, there appeared to be increased job satisfaction for management accountants, especially after the ERP system was operating for a period of time. Some organisations reported a reduction in staff turnover after the implementation of the ERP system.

All interviewees were consistent in their perception of the skills needed by management accountants in an ERP environment. In addition to traditional technical accounting skills, they emphasised the importance of communication skills, interpersonal skills, presentation skills, leadership skills, decision-making ability and being able to understand the business.

Despite the many million pounds these organisations had spent on their ERP projects, very little evidence of formal ongoing monitoring of the ERP investment decision was found. Formal post-implementation benefit assessment was also absent in most of the organisations; and none of the organisations appear to have undertaken any formal post-implementation review. In some cases, it was as if they assumed their ERP system would be ok in the end and wanted to avoid formally quantifying benefits and impacts so as to avoid recognising any of the issues that were arising other than those they could not ignore.

Illustrating that point, the impacts of the ERP systems appeared to be being monitored reactively rather than proactively; and there was a lack of continuous monitoring of ERP system use. However, managers are noticing the reactions of management accountants and other users to the ERP systems and are aware of what has worked and what has not, and of the impact that the implementation has had upon morale and working practices amongst the management accountants. However, little appears to be being done to bring less enthusiastic management accountants into line. As a result, many management accountants are continuing to use spreadsheets and other software for their reports, opening the way for corporate governance and Sarbanes–Oxley issues over data integrity. Despite this obvious problem, there was a noticeable lack of effective education and support for users, particularly in the less successful implementations.

Participants also provided insight and advice that they would offer to management accountants of other organisations implementing and using ERP systems and what they would recommend as 'best practices.' The advice varied from software advice to business advice.

Appendix 2

Mail Out Letter Sent with Postal Questionnaire

7th January 2004
Dear

1. **A NEW CIMA REPORT ON IMPROVING DECISION MAKING IN YOUR ORGANISATION**
2. **CIMA COMMISSIONED RESEARCH ON THE CHANGING ROLE OF MANAGEMENT ACCOUNTING**

I have pleasure in enclosing a copy of the latest CIMA executive report entitled *Improving Decision Making in your Organisation*. This report shares some of the learning gained from the CIMA Strategic Enterprise Management Round Table, which has included the finance directors and controllers of a number of large companies including Unilever, Roche, BBC, Royal Mail, Allied Domecq, and Powergen along with case study participants from companies including Shell, Rolls Royce, Lloyds TSB and the Inland Revenue.

You have probably heard of the term Strategic Enterprise Management, Business Performance Management and Business Intelligence from a number of enterprise software vendors. From our perspective, all these approaches are aimed at allowing the executive board and senior management time to focus primarily on high level strategic issues by empowering the management team(s) and the staff of existing operations to run them on a day to day basis. This requires systems and processes that will allow all involved to have the right information with sufficient quality and integrity (a single version of the truth) upon which to make good decisions and monitor performance.

This report focuses on the finance function's perspective of improving decision making. CIMA SEM is mainly about enhancing the role of the finance function and management accounting to add value constantly as part of the management team by taking a value creation perspective and properly integrating advanced management accounting techniques and then supporting them by enabling technologies.

We have considered how individual organisations have approached the key aspects of improving decision making. These are explored in more detail in the report and include:

- Managing for value
- Improving the process of decision making

- Strategic orientation of finance professionals
- Understanding the business model and effective performance measurement
- Utilisation of technologies to facilitate the process of operational empowerment

We hope you will find the report useful and thought provoking. Please do not hesitate to contact me to discuss any aspects of the SEM project and our proposed benchmarking initiative (see page 25 of the report for detail). Your colleagues can download their own copies at the following web address: http://www.cimaglobal.com/sem.

Finally, it is important for our members that we continue to research the impact of enterprise wide systems on the perspectives of management accountants and, in particular, the impact of the integration of ERP systems and management accounting techniques. To this end, please find enclosed some further information about a research project being conducted by Professor Leech of the University of Melbourne, Professor Grabski of Michigan State University and Professor Sangster of the Open University Business School, along with a short questionnaire and reply paid envelope for its return. You will also find three sealed envelopes. Please pass these to colleagues whose position most closely matches the descriptions on the front of those envelopes.

We would be extremely grateful if you could spend the 20 to 30 minutes required to complete the questionnaire. Following analysis of the survey results and follow-up interview-based case studies of six companies (which will be arranged separately), we will feed back the findings to those who request a summary of the results when completing the questionnaire.

Yours sincerely

Stathis Gould

Stathis Gould
Head of Technical Issues
stathis.gould@cimaglobal.com

Appendix 3

Information Sheet Sent with Postal Questionnaire

Information sheet

Project Title:
Management Accountants and Enterprise Resource Planning Systems

Project Sponsor:
The Chartered Institute of Management Accountants ("**CIMA**"), 26 Chapter Street, London, SW1P 4NP

Investigators:

Professor Stewart Leech	Professor Severin Grabski	Professor Alan Sangster
The University of Melbourne	Michigan State University	Open University Business School
Email: saleech@unimelb.edu.au	Email: grabski@pilot.msu.edu	Email: a.sangster@open.ac.uk

Purpose:
The aim of this project is to determine the changes made and the changes required by the implementation of enterprise resource planning (ERP) systems on the work and behaviour of management accountants. By examining the changes made and the changes deemed required by management accountants, this study is critical to the effective use of ERP systems in this vital area of accounting. The study will provide advice to management accountants on the changes needed to achieve the most benefit from an ERP system implementation.

Procedures, Data Collection and Use:
This stage of data collection is by survey. The development of the questionnaire was informed by the current literature and information collected in pilot studies conducted by Professors Sangster and Leech in three organisations in the UK. Once the survey data has been collected and analysed, it is intended to conduct intensive interviews with three or more companies (who have identified themselves as willing to participate). The case studies will considerably enrich the data obtained through the survey.

We will protect your anonymity and the confidentiality of your responses to the fullest possible extent, within the limits of the law. Your contact details will be kept in a password-protected computer file that is kept completely separately from the data you provide. The link between these details and your responses will only be made by the researchers and only to ensure that the questionnaire has been returned to us. The data is processed without any identifying details attached, and is then completely anonymous. Once the study has been completed, a brief summary of the findings will be available to you from CIMA. The researchers will keep the data securely in password-protected computer files for five years from the date of publication before being destroyed.

Participation:
Your participation in this project is completely voluntary. Should you wish to withdraw at any stage, or to withdraw any unprocessed data you have supplied, you are free to do so without prejudice. If you are happy to participate, please return your completed questionnaire. Your participation is most important to our project and we hope that you have the time to complete the questionnaire.

Queries or Concerns:
Should you require any further information, or have any concerns, please do not hesitate to contact Professor Alan Sangster, Open University Business School, (email: a.sangster@open.ac.uk).

The project has ethical clearance from the administering university, the University of Melbourne. If you have concerns of an ethical nature, please contact The Executive Officer, Human Research Ethics, Office for Research and Innovation, The University of Melbourne, Victoria, 3010, Australia, telephone: +61 3 8344 4071 or fax: +61 3 9347 6739.

Appendix 4

Postal Questionnaire Survey Instrument

Management Accountants and Enterprise Resource Planning Systems

If your organisation has not acquired an enterprise resource planning ("ERP") system, please tick this box and go directly to PART III. ☐

PART I. ENTERPRISE RESOURCE PLANNING BUSINESS IMPACT

1. Which of the following ERP ("Enterprise Resource Planning") packages did your organisation implement? (Please tick)

   ☐ Baan   ☐ J D Edwards   ☐ Oracle   ☐ PeopleSoft   ☐ SAP
   ☐ Other (please specify) _____

2. This question relates to the ERP system modules that have been implemented. <u>Please tick or enter the name of each module in use, one per line, and then complete the three columns concerning period in use, extent of usage and success.</u>

   In the "Extent of use in organisation" column (A), please state your opinion of how much the module has been used relative to the full extent of its known capabilities. (Please fill in your answer using a scale of 0% - 100%, where 0% means the module has not been used and 100% means the module has been used to full capacity.) In the "Success" column (B), please state your opinion of how successful the implementation of each module is. (Please use a scale of 1-7, where *1* means the implementation is *very unsuccessful* i.e. the module is not functional at all, 4 is neutral i.e. neither successful nor unsuccessful, and *7* means the implementation is *very successful*.)

	ERP Modules Implemented	In use for				(A) Extent of use in organisation (%)	(B) Success
		months		years			
✓	Example	6	months	2	years	75%	5
	Financials & G/L		months		years		
	Sales & A/R		months		years		
	Purchasing & A/P		months		years		
	Distribution		months		years		
	HR ("Human Resource")		months		years		
	Manufacturing		months		years		
	Warehouse		months		years		
	Other (please specify)						
	1.		months		years		
	2.		months		years		
	3.		months		years		

Please turn over →

3. Were you involved in the implementation of the ERP system? (Please tick)

☐ Yes   ☐ No

If yes, please specify: (i) The period of your involvement: Begin _____ End _____

(ii) The nature of your involvement:

_____

4. In your opinion, has the ERP system been a success? (Please circle)

1	2	3	4	5	6	7	don't know
Very unsuccessful			**Neutral**			**Very successful**	

5. Do you think that senior management believe the ERP system to be a success? (Please circle)

1	2	3	4	5	6	7	don't know
Very unsuccessful			**Neutral**			**Very successful**	

6. In your opinion, to what extent is the ERP system able to support the core competencies of your organisation's business? (Please circle)

1	2	3	4	5	6	7	don't know
Not at all			**Supports about half**			**Supports all**	

7. In your opinion, what was the extent of changes in business processes in your organisation just before, during, or after implementation of the ERP system? (Please circle)

	None			Moderate		Extensive		
a. Just before ERP system implementation	1	2	3	4	5	6	7	don't know
b. During ERP system implementation	1	2	3	4	5	6	7	don't know
c. After ERP system implementation	1	2	3	4	5	6	7	don't know

8. To what extent do you agree with the following descriptions of your organisational culture? (Please circle)

	Agree					Disagree		
a. All decisions are made exclusively by senior management who are in total control	1	2	3	4	5	6	7	don't know
b. Flexible and open to employees' suggestions	1	2	3	4	5	6	7	don't know

9. To what extent does your organisational culture succeed in motivating the employees to accept and use the ERP system? (Please circle)

1	2	3	4	5	6	7	don't know
Very unsuccessful			**Neutral**			**Very successful**	

10. To what extent have cost savings resulted from the ERP system? (Please circle)

1	2	3	4	5	6	7	don't know
Significant costs incurred			**No savings nor increased costs**			**Significant cost savings**	

11. To what extent has more timely information resulted from the ERP system? (Please circle)

1	2	3	4	5	6	7	don't know
Significant delays incurred			**No change in information timeliness**			**Significant improvement**	

12. To what extent has better quality information resulted from the ERP system? (Please circle)

1	2	3	4	5	6	7	don't know
Significant deterioration in information quality			**No change in information quality**			**Significant improvement in information quality**	

13. To what extent did senior management support the project? (Please circle)

1	2	3	4	5	6	7	don't know
Fully opposed			**Neutral**			**Fully supported**	

14. Please tick one box for the ERP system and one box for the organisational structure

☐ ERP system is **process** oriented ☐ Organisational structure is **process** oriented

☐ ERP system is **business function** oriented ☐ Organisational structure is **business function** oriented

15. To what extent do the ERP system and the organisational structure match? (Please circle)

1	2	3	4	5	6	7	don't know
Do not match			**Neutral**			**Match completely**	

16. ERP module training provided: (Please circle)

	None		Moderate			Extensive		
a. Training for all employees	1	2	3	4	5	6	7	don't know
b. Training for key personnel	1	2	3	4	5	6	7	don't know
c. Training for yourself	1	2	3	4	5	6	7	don't know

17. In your opinion, did the employees take ownership of the *system implementation*? (Please circle)

1	2	3	4	5	6	7	don't know
No ownership			**Neutral**			**Complete ownership**	

18. In your opinion, did the employees take ownership in using the *operational ERP system*? (Please circle)

1	2	3	4	5	6	7	don't know
No ownership			**Neutral**			**Complete ownership**	

19. Is it easy for the employees to get the ERP system to do what they want? (Please circle)

1	2	3	4	5	6	7	don't know
Very easy			**Neutral**			**Very difficult**	

20. What are the major job changes that have resulted from the implementation of the ERP system?

_____

_____

21. In your opinion, has the ERP system been a success in terms of performance measures adopted by your organisation to measure its success? (Please circle)

	Very unsuccessful			**Neutral**			**Very successful**	
a. When initially implemented	1	2	3	4	5	6	7	don't know
b. Currently	1	2	3	4	5	6	7	don't know

Please turn over →

22. In your opinion, to what extent has the ERP system affected the following? (Please circle)

		Significant adverse effect			No change			Significant improvement	
a.	Inventory levels	1	2	3	4	5	6	7	don't know
b.	Order management and cycle times	1	2	3	4	5	6	7	don't know
c.	Procurement costs	1	2	3	4	5	6	7	don't know
d.	Inventory turnaround time	1	2	3	4	5	6	7	don't know
e.	Overall operation costs	1	2	3	4	5	6	7	don't know
f.	On-time delivery	1	2	3	4	5	6	7	don't know
g.	Productivity	1	2	3	4	5	6	7	don't know
h.	Ability of the organisation to respond to change	1	2	3	4	5	6	7	don't know
i.	Ability to conduct e-commerce	1	2	3	4	5	6	7	don't know
j.	Cash management	1	2	3	4	5	6	7	don't know
k.	Customer service	1	2	3	4	5	6	7	don't know
l.	Decision-making and planning	1	2	3	4	5	6	7	don't know
m.	Information/Data quality in general	1	2	3	4	5	6	7	don't know
n.	Other (please specify): _____	1	2	3	4	5	6	7	don't know

PART II. THE ROLE OF MANAGEMENT ACCOUNTANT(S)

1. What role did the management accountant(s) play in the implementation of the ERP system? (Management accountants are broadly defined and include not only accountants that provide, analyse and communicate information but also project accountants or internal business consulting accountants that play a part in helping to manage the business.)

   _____
   _____

2. What is the percentage increase (decrease) in number of management accountants as a result of the implementation of the ERP system?

   ____ % Increase   ____ % Decrease   ____ Don't know

3. Was there any initial resistance from the management accountants relating to the use of the ERP system? (Please tick)

   ☐ Yes   ☐ No   ☐ Don't know

4. Please indicate the extent to which you believe the ERP system has had an impact on the roles of management accountant(s) in your organisation as highlighted below (Please circle)

		Very much reduced			No change			Very much increased	
a.	Time spent on data collection	1	2	3	4	5	6	7	don't know
b.	Time spent on data analysis	1	2	3	4	5	6	7	don't know
c.	Involvement in business decision making	1	2	3	4	5	6	7	don't know
d.	Focus on internal reporting (e.g. performance measurement and control issues)	1	2	3	4	5	6	7	don't know
e.	Focus on external environment (e.g. benchmarking)	1	2	3	4	5	6	7	don't know

5. What other changes in the management accountant's role have resulted from the implementation of the ERP system?

   _____
   _____

6. In your opinion, what are the benefits or improvements accrued in the management accounting system as a result of the ERP system (if any)?

_____
_____

7. In your opinion, what disadvantages or problems occurred in the management accounting system as a result of the implementation of the ERP system (if any)?

_____
_____

8. In your opinion, what are the changes in the use of the following as a result of the implementation of the ERP system? (Please circle)

		Reduced extensively			No change			Increased extensively	
a.	Financial and non-financial performance measure models e.g. the Balanced Scorecard	1	2	3	4	5	6	7	don't know
b.	Activity Based Costing	1	2	3	4	5	6	7	don't know
c.	Management Controls	1	2	3	4	5	6	7	don't know
d.	Supply Chain Management techniques	1	2	3	4	5	6	7	don't know
e.	Use of Strategic Management software	1	2	3	4	5	6	7	don't know
f.	Generation of forward looking reports	1	2	3	4	5	6	7	don't know

9. What management accounting procedures are performed outside the ERP system (e.g. Activity Based Costing, Balanced Scorecard, the use of excel spreadsheets for report generation)? Why?

_____
_____

10. To what extent are reports that were formerly generated by the management accountant, either manually or using the prior system, now either automatically generated by the ERP system or by managers using the ERP system?

_____ **Percentage former reports now generated by the ERP system or by managers using the ERP system**

11. Overall, to what extent do you believe that the ERP system had an impact on the following? (Please circle)

		Significant negative impact			No significant change			Significant positive impact	
a.	Management accounting in general	1	2	3	4	5	6	7	don't know
b.	Role of the management accountant(s)	1	2	3	4	5	6	7	don't know
c.	Role of line managers with accounting knowledge	1	2	3	4	5	6	7	don't know

12. Overall, to what extent do you believe that the ERP system had an impact on the following? (Please circle)

		Significant decrease			No significant change			Significant increase	
a.	Communication across functional areas	1	2	3	4	5	6	7	don't know
b.	Number of routine accounting jobs	1	2	3	4	5	6	7	don't know
c.	Forward looking information	1	2	3	4	5	6	7	don't know
d.	Breadth of role for management accounting	1	2	3	4	5	6	7	don't know

13. What different skills do management accountants need as a result of the ERP system implementation? (Please circle)

		Much less			No change			Much more	
a.	Communication skills	1	2	3	4	5	6	7	don't know
b.	Interpersonal skills	1	2	3	4	5	6	7	don't know
c.	Broad-based business knowledge	1	2	3	4	5	6	7	don't know
d.	Technical accounting skills	1	2	3	4	5	6	7	don't know
e.	Technical ERP skills	1	2	3	4	5	6	7	don't know
f.	Consulting skills	1	2	3	4	5	6	7	don't know
g.	Cross-functional working relationships	1	2	3	4	5	6	7	don't know

Please turn over →

14. Please circle the appropriate response in the column to the right

I COULD COMPLETE MY JOB USING THE ERP SOFTWARE PACKAGE:	Not at all confident								Completely confident	
if there was no one around to tell me what to do	1	2	3	4	5	6	7	8	9	10
if I had only the software manuals for reference	1	2	3	4	5	6	7	8	9	10
if I had a lot of time to complete the job for which the software was provided	1	2	3	4	5	6	7	8	9	10
if I had seen someone else using it before trying it myself	1	2	3	4	5	6	7	8	9	10
if someone else had helped me get started	1	2	3	4	5	6	7	8	9	10
if I could call someone for help if I got stuck	1	2	3	4	5	6	7	8	9	10
if I had just the built-in help facility for assistance	1	2	3	4	5	6	7	8	9	10
if someone showed me how to do it first	1	2	3	4	5	6	7	8	9	10

IN MY JOB AS A MANAGEMENT ACCOUNTANT:	Agree completely						Disagree completely
I have a clear idea of what someone in my job does	1	2	3	4	5	6	7
The job provides a total fit for me	1	2	3	4	5	6	7
My superiors expect me to use the ERP system	1	2	3	4	5	6	7
I work under incompatible policies and guidelines	1	2	3	4	5	6	7
My supervisor encourages the use of the ERP system	1	2	3	4	5	6	7
I consider the new ERP system to be relevant to me	1	2	3	4	5	6	7
I have a very good idea of what my job entails	1	2	3	4	5	6	7
My interaction with the ERP system is clear and understandable	1	2	3	4	5	6	7
I would prefer another, more ideal job	1	2	3	4	5	6	7
Using the ERP system increases the level of challenge in my job	1	2	3	4	5	6	7
I felt my opinion was adequately considered during the process of design and/or development of the ERP system	1	2	3	4	5	6	7
I think that using the ERP system fits well with the way I like to work	1	2	3	4	5	6	7
I am well aware of the duties that are required of me	1	2	3	4	5	6	7
I am proud to tell others that I am part of this organisation	1	2	3	4	5	6	7
Using the ERP system enables me to accomplish tasks more quickly	1	2	3	4	5	6	7
I consider that the new ERP system means a lot to me	1	2	3	4	5	6	7
My supervisor requires me to use the system	1	2	3	4	5	6	7
Due to the ERP system, I have to do things that I believe should be done differently	1	2	3	4	5	6	7
Using the ERP system increases the opportunity for preferred career assignments	1	2	3	4	5	6	7
I find it easy to get the ERP system to do what I want it to do	1	2	3	4	5	6	7
I am proud to tell others that I am part of this profession	1	2	3	4	5	6	7
Using the ERP system significantly increases the quality of output from my job	1	2	3	4	5	6	7
I work on unnecessary things	1	2	3	4	5	6	7
My use of the ERP system is voluntary	1	2	3	4	5	6	7

IN MY JOB AS A MANAGEMENT ACCOUNTANT:	Agree completely					Disagree completely
I played an important role in the design and/or development of the ERP system	1	2	3	4	5	6	7
Using the ERP system increases the effectiveness of performing job tasks	1	2	3	4	5	6	7
I consider the new ERP system to be of no concern to me	1	2	3	4	5	6	7
My manager discourages the use of the ERP system	1	2	3	4	5	6	7
Using the ERP system enhances my effectiveness on the job	1	2	3	4	5	6	7
Interacting with the ERP system does not require a lot of mental effort	1	2	3	4	5	6	7
I participated in the design and/or development of the ERP system	1	2	3	4	5	6	7
I am satisfied with the important aspects of my job	1	2	3	4	5	6	7
Using the ERP system has no effect on the performance of my job	1	2	3	4	5	6	7
I talk up this profession to my friends as a great profession	1	2	3	4	5	6	7
I consider the new ERP system to be significant to me	1	2	3	4	5	6	7
Using the ERP system decreases the time needed for my important job responsibilities	1	2	3	4	5	6	7
Overall, I am satisfied with my job	1	2	3	4	5	6	7
Using the ERP system is compatible with all aspects of my work	1	2	3	4	5	6	7
Using the system increases the flexibility of changing jobs	1	2	3	4	5	6	7
I fit right into the job since the ERP implementation	1	2	3	4	5	6	7
Although it might be helpful, using the ERP system is certainly not compulsory in my job	1	2	3	4	5	6	7
I find the ERP system to be hard to use	1	2	3	4	5	6	7
Using the ERP system increases my opportunity to gain job security	1	2	3	4	5	6	7
I talk up this organisation to my friends as a great organisation to work for	1	2	3	4	5	6	7
Using the ERP system fits into my work style	1	2	3	4	5	6	7
The use of the ERP system is encouraged by management	1	2	3	4	5	6	7
I feel a sense of belonging to this profession rather than it just being a job	1	2	3	4	5	6	7
Using the ERP system makes it harder to do my job	1	2	3	4	5	6	7
Taking everything into account, the job is a complete fit for me	1	2	3	4	5	6	7
Using the ERP system increases the amount of variety in my career	1	2	3	4	5	6	7
The ERP system can increase the quantity of output for the same amount of effort	1	2	3	4	5	6	7
Using the ERP system increases the opportunity for more meaningful work	1	2	3	4	5	6	7
I feel a sense of "ownership" for this organisation rather than just being an employee	1	2	3	4	5	6	7

Please turn over →

Part III. DEMOGRAPHICS

1. What is the primary line of business in your organisation? _____
2. Where is the location of your office? _____
3. Does your organisation have several locations in the UK? ☐ Yes ☐ No
4. Is the same ERP system used at all the locations in the UK? ☐ Yes ☐ No ☐ Don't know
5. Does your organisation have an established office outside UK? ☐ Yes ☐ No
6. Approximately what is the market share that your organisation has in the industry in the UK? ____ %
7. Approximately how many <u>major</u> competitors does your organisation have in the industry in the UK? ____
8. What is your current job title? _____
9. How long have you been in this position? ____ years ____ months
10. How many years have you held a senior management position? ____ years ____ months
11. Ignoring any changes in your organisation's name or structure, for how many years have you worked in your current organisation? ____ years ____ months

---

Thank you for taking the time to complete this questionnaire. If you would like a summary of the results, please enter your name and address below:

Name _____
Organisation _____
Address _____
_____
_____
_____

OR ATTACH BUSINESS CARD

Names and addresses supplied here will be stored separately from any data provided and only used to send out summaries of the results once the project is completed.

If you would be willing to be interviewed about your experiences with the ERP system (which is the second phase of this CIMA-funded project), please enter a daytime telephone number or email address here:

Email: _____
Telephone: _____

OR ATTACH BUSINESS CARD

Thank you for taking the time to complete this questionnaire.
Please return it to Professor Alan Sangster, The Open University Business School, Walton Hall, Milton Keynes, MK7 6AA in the reply paid envelope provided

For internal use only

Appendix 5

Information Sheet Used in Case Study Interviews

THE UNIVERSITY OF MELBOURNE

Department of Accounting and Business Information Systems
Victoria 3010 Australia
Tel: +61 3 8344 5314

Research Project:
Management Accounting in Enterprise Resource Planning Systems

INFORMATION SHEET

Project Title:
Management Accounting in Enterprise Resource Planning Systems

Project Sponsor:
The Chartered Institute Of Management Accountants ("**CIMA**"), 26 Chapter Street, London, SW1P 4NP

Investigators:

Professor Stewart Leech	Professor Severin Grabski	Professor Alan Sangster
The University of Melbourne	Michigan State University	Robert Gordon University
Email: saleech@unimelb.edu.au	Email: grabski@pilot.msu.edu	Email: a.j.a.sangster@rgu.ac.uk

Purpose:
The aim of this project is to determine the changes made and the changes required by the implementation of enterprise resource planning (ERP) systems on the work and behaviour of management accountants. By examining the changes made and the changes deemed required by management accountants, this study is critical to the effective use of ERP systems in this vital area of accounting. The study will provide advice to management accountants on the changes needed to achieve the most benefit from an ERP system implementation.

Procedures, Data Collection and Use:

In-depth semi-structured interviews and discussions with Management Accountants (and others where appropriate, for example Chief information Officers, Chief Financial Officers, Business Managers, IT Analysts) will be used for gathering data. Professors Leech and Sangster will conduct the interviews, which are planned to be of about 60 minutes duration. The semi-structured interviews will be conducted in a free-flowing manner, and the investigators will provide a forum that encourages executives to discuss relevant information. With permission, the interview will be tape-recorded to gain an accurate record and subsequently transcribed. You are assured of complete confidentiality. The data will be stored in secure places (locked filing cabinets, password protected computer files). Neither you nor your organisation will be identified directly in any publications that may arise from the research. Any references to the information you provide will be referred to only by a pseudonym that will not allow identification of you or your organisation. Please note that the confidentiality of information provided can only be protected within the limitations of the law.

Participation:

Participation in this research is entirely voluntary. Participants can withdraw at any time and withdraw any data.

Queries or Concerns:

If you have any queries or concerns about the research, please contact Professor Stewart Leech at the above address (email: saleech@unimelb.edu.au) or telephone +61 3 8344 5314.

If you have concerns of an ethical nature, please contact The Executive Officer, Human Research Ethics, Office for Research and Innovation, The University of Melbourne, Victoria, 3010, Australia, telephone +61 3 8344 4071 or fax +61 3 9347 6739.

Appendix 6

Case Study Interview Script

Case Studies September 2004 Interview Script

Background Information

Company Name
Participant's Name
Position/Title
Prior Work Experience

Package implemented? Modules implemented? – Might be able to get this from survey

How long has the ERP system been operational?

Q14 & Q15 from the first questionnaire survey need to be clarified (need to clarify "Process" and "Business Function") in the interview.

14. Please tick one box for the ERP system and one box for the organisational structure

    ☐ ERP system is *process* oriented   ☐ Organisational structure is *process* oriented

    ☐ ERP system is *business function* oriented ☐ Organisational structure is *business function* oriented

15. To what extent do the ERP system and the organisational structure match? (Please circle)

          1   2 3   4 5 6   7   *don't know*

    Do not match   **Neutral**   **Match completely**

General Questions

Implementation Activities:

Involvement in implementation of ERP package
   Were you actively involved in the installation of the ERP package? How? What did you do? What was your role?

If the participant is not an MA, should ask questions about the MA:
   Involvement in implementation of ERP package

During the installation and subsequent use of the ERP system, tell us what happened, why it happened, and what do you expect in the future.

What would you (MA) do differently/the same knowing everything that you know now after the ERP implementation?

ERP System Evaluation:

Is the ERP implementation a success?
Based upon what metrics?
From whose perspective?

Current Use of ERP Software by the MA

Current amount of work performed:
   Directly using the ERP package
   Using reports generated by the ERP package
   What work is performed not using ERP package?
   What percentage/amount of work is not affected by the ERP package?

What can be done now that you could not do before?
What can't you do now that you did before?

What, if any, was the "defining moment" (the "A-HA" moment) either in the implementation or use of the ERP package when you (the MA) realized the value/issues with the ERP environment?

How has the Job of the Management Accountant Changed?

In general, how has the role of the MA in the organisation changed since the ERP system implementation?

Has there been any reduction (increase) in the number of MAs due to the implementation of the ERP system?

How has the role of the MA changed with respect to data analysis? (Q4 questions in Part II need clarification and expansion).

		Very much reduced		No change		Very much increased		
	Please indicate the extent to which you believe the ERP system has had an impact on the roles of management accountant(s) in your organisation as highlighted below (Please circle)								
a.	Time spent on data collection	1	2	3	4	5	6	7	don't know
b.	Time spent on data analysis	1	2	3	4	5	6	7	don't know
c.	Involvement in business decision making	1	2	3	4	5	6	7	don't know
d.	Focus on internal reporting (e.g. performance measurement and control issues)	1	2	3	4	5	6	7	don't know
e.	Focus on external environment (e.g. benchmarking)	1	2	3	4	5	6	7	don't know

To what extent are traditional analyses performed that focus on past operating results compared to decision support type of analyses that have a forward-looking focus?

Are there cross-functional analyses versus domain specific analyses?

Since less time is needed for data capture, and less time is spent generating routine reports for managers, what are you (the MA) doing with the extra time?

Has the formal or informal communication structure involving the MAs changed as a result of the implementation of the ERP system?

How satisfied are you with your job, both prior to and post-ERP implementation?

How has the MA contributed to the success of the ERP system?

Recommendations for Management Accountants

What skills would you recommend for MAs in organisations that have recently implemented ERP systems?

Are there any **new** skills you recommend for MAs? (What are they?)
What skills that you currently use have become more important?

What skills did you use prior to ERP implementation that you do not use (as much?) now?

What would you recommend as a 'Best Practices' for other MAs?
'Worst Practices?'

How should MAs use ERP systems?

If you were presenting a seminar for MAs in firms that have just implemented an ERP system, what type of guidance would you provide to them?

Index

A

Accountants, and BAAN system implementation (Case F), 73–76
  impact on role of, 74–76
  role of, 73
  use of systems, 73–74
Accountants, and ERP systems implementation, 93–94
  education program, 99–100
  guidance, 95–98
  impact on role of, 104–110, 118–120
  impact on work of, 113–115
  monitoring, 98–99
  post-implementation issues, 100–101
  skills required, 110–113
Accountants, and JD Edwards system implementation (Case A)
  Chart of Accounts, 17–18
  impact on role of, 19–22
  information systems and, 19
  recommendations for, 22–23
  role of, 18
Accountants, and SAP implementation (Case B), 28–33
  impact on role of, 28–30
  problems of, 26
  recommendations for, 32–33
  role of, 28
  training of, 27
  use of systems by, 28
Accountants, and SAP implementation (Case C)
  impact on role of, 39–41
  recommendations for, 42–44
  reporting, 39
  role of, 38
  success of, 41–42
  use of systems, 39
Accountants, and SAP implementation (Case D)
  impact on role of, 47–50
  recommendations for, 51–52
  role of, 46
  success, 50
  use of systems, 46
Accountants, and SAP implementation (Case E), 57–64
  impact on role of, 58–63
  recommendations for, 63–64
  role of, 57
  successful implementation, 62–63
  use of systems by, 57–58
Accountants, and SAP implementation (Case G), 79–83
  impact on role of, 80–82
  recommendations for, 83
  role of, 79–80
  successful implementation, 82–83
Analytical skills, of accountants, 112
Audio and telecommunications company (Case C), SAP implementation in
  accountants, 38–44
  cost savings, 36
  key champions of, 36–37
  level of success of, 38
  modules, 35
  outsourcing transaction processing, 37–38
  rollout phases, 36
  strategy, 35
  team for, 36
Automotive company, BAAN system implementation in (Case F)
  accountants, 73–76
  business overview, 66
  business process reengineering, 67
  duration of, 66
  e-commerce, 73
  impact on company, 68–71
  modules of, 66
  problems, 72–73
  project team in, 66–67
  and success of modules, 71–72
  target methodology of, 68
  training, 67

Index

B
BAAN system implementation (Case F)
  accountants, 73–76
  business overview, 66
  business process reengineering, 67
  duration of, 66
  e-commerce, 73
  impact on company, 68–71
  modules of, 66
  problems, 72–73
  project team in, 66–67
  success of modules and, 71–72
  target methodology of, 68
  training, 67
Benefits, ERP systems implementation, 1–2.
  See also Success factors, ERP systems implementation
Best of Breed (BoB) systems, 9–10
BoB systems. *See* Best of Breed (BoB) systems
Budget control, 119
Business decision-making, accountants' involvement in, 105
Business process re-engineering, 6

C
Case studies, on ERP system implementation
  Case A, 17–23
  Case B, 24–34
  Case C, 35–44
  Case D, 45–52
  Case E, 53–64
  Case F, 66–76
  Case G, 77–83
  information sheet for, 141–142
  interview script, 143–145
  lessons, 85–88
  summary, 127–128
Chart of Accounts, 17–18, 46
Communication skills, of accountants, 109, 112
Communication structure, 109
Complementarity theory, 7
Control theory, 7
Correspondence failure, 8
Cost-benefit analysis, of ERP systems implementation, 90
Costs, of ERP systems implementation, 6, 90
Cross-functional analysis, and accountants, 106–107

D
Data analysis, time spent on, 105
Data collection, time spent on, 104–105

Data governance framework, 115
Data model development, 114
Data quality management programme, 115
Data stewardship, 115
Decision-making skills, of accountants, 112
Dell Computers, 6

E
Education program, for ERP systems implementation, 99–100
Educator skills, of accountants, 112
Energy and aerospace company, SAP implementation in (Case G)
  accountant and, 79–83
  business overview, 77
  corporate reporting, 79
  ledger accounts creation, 78–79
  modules, 77–78
  project team, 77
  successful aspects of, 79
Enterprise resource planning (ERP) systems implementation
  accountants. *See* Accountants, and ERP systems implementation
  advantages of, 90
  benefits of, 1–2
  case studies on. *See* Case studies, on ERP systems implementation
  cost-benefit analysis of, 90
  failure factors, 7–8
  impact on accounting, 8–11
  implementation success, 11–12
  integration across business divisions, 90
  motivation for, 89–91
  research methodology, 13–14
  success factor, 6–7, 90–91
  Y2K crises, 5
Entrepreneurial salesman skills, 111
ERP. *See* Enterprise resource planning (ERP) systems implementation
Excel spreadsheet, 18. *See also* Spreadsheets
Expectation failure, 7
External environment, and accountants, 106

F
Failure factors, 7–8
Food and consumer products company, SAP implementation in (Case E)
  accountants, 57–64
  back office activities, 54
  cost, 56–57
  end user decision support, 54

Index 149

initial process, 53, 57
modifications (revised system), 55, 56
R&D site, 53–54
web interface, 53
Food services and beverage company, SAP implementation in (Case D)
    accountants, 46–52
    Chart of Accounts, 46
    initial process of, 45
    overview of business, 45
    reengineering, 46
Forward-looking analysis, and accountants, 106
FoxMeyer Drugs, 6

G

Guidance, for accountants, 95–98

H

Heavy-engineering/chemicals company (Case B)
    accountants, 27, 28–33
    legacy systems, 24–25
    SAP systems implementation. *See* SAP systems, implementation (Case B)

I

IFRS reporting, 113–114
Information sheet, 131–132
    for case studies, 141–142
Information technology, business, 6
Internal reporting, and accountants, 105
Interview script, for case studies, 143–145
Investment decisions, monitoring of, 98

J

JD Edwards (JDE) system implementation (Case A)
    accountants, 18–23
    business overview, 17
    Chart of Accounts, 17–18
    reasons of success, 18
Job satisfaction, of accountants, 109–110

L

Leadership skills, of accountants, 112

M

Management Consultants. *See* Heavy-engineering/chemicals company (Case B)
Monitoring
    impacts of ERP system implementation, 98–99
    investment decisions, 98

O

Organisational change programs, 9

P

Performance measurement and management (PMM), 9
Planning skills, of accountants, 112
PMM. *See* Performance measurement and management (PMM)
Postal questionnaire
    case study interview information sheet, 141–142
    case study interview script, 143–145
    information sheet, 131–132
    mail out letter, 129–130
    survey instrument, 133–140
Post-implementation, of ERP systems
    benefits, 100
    review, 100–101
Process failure, 7

Q

Questionnaire. *See* Postal questionnaire

R

Research methodology, 13–14
Risk factors, 8

S

SAP implementation (Case C)
    accountants, 38–44
    cost savings, 36
    key champions of, 36–37
    level of success of, 38
    modules, 35
    outsourcing transaction processing, 37–38
    rollout phases, 36
    strategy, 35
    team for, 36
SAP implementation (Case D)
    accountants, 46–52
    Chart of Accounts, 46
    initial process of, 45
    overview of business, 45
    reengineering, 46
SAP implementation (Case E)
    accountants, 57–64
    back office activities, 54
    cost, 56–57
    end user decision support, 54
    initial process, 53, 57
    modifications (revised system), 55, 56

SAP implementation (Case E) (*Continued*)
  R&D site, 53–54
  web interface, 53
SAP implementation (Case G)
  accountant and, 79–83
  business overview, 77
  corporate reporting, 79
  ledger accounts creation, 78–79
  modules, 77–78
  project team, 77
  successful aspects of, 79
SAP systems, implementation (Case B)
  and accountants, 28–33
  challenges/decisions, 25–27
  decision making, 25
  training to accountants, 27
Sarbanes-Oxley (SOX) Act of 2002, 113
SEM. *See* Strategic enterprise management (SEM)
Skills, of accountants in ERP environment, 110–113, 118–119
Spreadsheets, 2, 18, 113, 114
Strategic enterprise management (SEM), 9
Success factors, ERP systems implementation, 6–7, 90–91

T

Technical skills, of accountants, 112
Telecommunications company, JD Edwards (JDE) system implementation (Case A)
  accountants, 18–23
  business overview, 17
  Chart of Accounts, 17–18
  reasons of success, 18
Time, 119
  on data analysis, 105
  on data collection, 104–105
  use of, 107–108

Y

Y2K crises, 5

LaVergne, TN USA
21 November 2009

164868LV00004B/44/P